LANGUAGE
OF THE LINES

LANGUAGE OF THE LINES

The I Ching Oracle

Nigel Richmond

Wildwood House London

First published 1977
Copyright © 1977 by Nigel Richmond

Wildwood House Ltd
29 King Street
London WC2

ISBN Hardback 0 7045 0299 2
Paperback 0 7045 0298 4

Set by Santype International (Coldtype Division)
Salisbury, Wiltshire

Printed and bound by Biddles Ltd, Guildford, Surrey

CONTENTS

PART ONE

*The Language and the
I Ching Oracle*

AN IMAGE OF REALITY

When an oracle maker begins to work he must look at the essence of reality in the same way that a wood carver examines the grain of wood, for the direction it will lead him in its depth. On the surface an oracle predicts the behaviour of reality, but beneath this appearance is a nature we long to know with our intelligence as well as our love of being.

The I Ching line language recognizes that there is a self-contained pattern of reality in the way binary lines may be combined together. It then recognizes that all reality states have a basic similarity of pattern and uses the binary framework as a language for the patterns reality takes in a more general sense. Thus it serves as a handle by which we can pick up our own reality and look at it with our minds. It should be clearly understood that we are not trying to compress reality into a conceptual framework but to expand the frame to accept greater reality: while forming a picture of reality, we must always guard against this image taking the place of the direct, dynamic experience of living without definition, which is the love of being.

We find ourselves in a seemingly complicated world we think of as our reality; it has overtones that there is more than this, or even that *all that is* is greater beyond our imagination. Our careful observations of this world show patterns which we have built into systems of logic in our sciences; one of the ways of doing this which has been fruitful is to suppose that a certain relationship exists and then to follow it to see what would be the logical result of its existence; then we see whether the picture this makes is useful to us.

To introduce a coherent picture reflecting reality I am going to put together two such suppositions: one is that the Chinese line language actually describes the way reality is and for that reason can be a true oracle of it; the other is that reality is not a possible idea at all unless there is *always* relativity. If these two ideas were held to be true what would our picture of reality be?

Firstly, what is relativity? At its simplest it is a statement that shut needs open, high needs low, objects need background, evil needs good, and so forth. These are polarities, differences which appear together like the two ends of a stick, and however often the stick is broken the two ends of each piece remain. So if reality is also relativity, it is these relationships of the whole and the ends that make anything real.

Matching this view of reality the line language of the I Ching oracle has a two-letter alphabet; the first letter is undivided, drawn ▬▬▬ and pronounced yang, while the second is divided, ▬▬ ▬▬ , pronounced yin.

These symbols represent two ways of experiencing the same thing; we can be one end of the stick as opposed to the other, or we can be the whole stick as opposed to something else.

Because we experience sequentially or 'one at a time', we come upon these two ways of seeing reality in turn and this gives it the appearance of coming in layers alternately whole and divided. When we think of breaking the stick, which is dividing it into ends, each time we do so we get a new stick (a new layer of reality) which also has two ends.

In our everyday world we are very aware of these ends of reality and we choose between them, making our consciousness a complex and moving pattern of polarities. If all these apparent opposites, like shut and open, were merged we would entirely lose our present viewpoint, and this viewpoint is our identity. By constantly choosing between polarities, liking and disliking, noticing and ignoring, our individuality is formed and in this way we continually choose our reality.

Relativity says that an idea such as high is impossible without there also being a low, so the two must be thought of as having a reality together, of being a whole, although we cannot know this whole while in our normal consciousness because we are constantly choosing amongst difference.

The way we act upon this difference is to focus on one end of it and ignore the other, to like one and hate the other or go towards one and away from the other: by continually choosing we have a conscious reality which divides and then identifies with one end of the division, ignoring or repelling its opposite. The actions which we avoid do not happen to us, they become a might-have-been reality, and as this is not in our conscious reality we feel that it does not exist. However, as we are supposing reality to be *always* relative this invisible side does exist in some way, but by choosing we have narrowed our awareness of *all that is* to exclude it. This is only to say that for a stick to be real both ends of it have to be real.

These chosen and disregarded parts of reality must be seen together as the whole stick of our reality, or rather this stick becomes the immediate layer where we have consciousness and unconsciousness. The word unconscious has been hard worked and under-defined, meaning many things to many people. I shall avoid it and use instead the sense that it is behind us and unseen because we have our two eyes at the front; so I shall call the conscious surface 'front' reality and the unconscious depth of this becomes the 'back'. These are also respectively the ▬ ▬ and ▬▬ of the line language.

So our front reality divides experience progressively into further layers of countless opposites amongst which we choose new paths; all these divisions are the front way of experiencing the stick of our reality, while the whole view of the stick, which we have to ignore, is the back.

In this idea back reality is not only the ignored part; it is the depth and has access to the dividing front reality also. This can be confusing because we are used to dividing experience into 'this' as opposed to 'that', not 'this' as opposed to 'this and that', but it is necessary to grasp the distinction firmly before we can see the key idea of the wholeness of *all that is* in its individuality.

So where we would usually divide experience into conscious and unconscious, the total of these is our back reality and the conscious part our front reality. These are ▬▬▬ and ▬▬ ▬▬ .

Together these have another reality (layer) which is ▬▬ ▬▬ / ▬▬▬ . We could roughly describe this as experiencing polarities together without each counteracting the other; when this happens there is experience of a reality layer wider than ▬▬ ▬▬ and ▬▬▬ .

In this way each of the reality layers we are visualizing slides into the next wider layer by already being part of it; *all that is* takes on the image of an infinite pyramid or gestalt which can have neither beginning nor end, and which is indivisibly one while at the same time being an infinity of identities. This infinite nature which we cannot encompass need not disturb us because it is only our way of thinking in sequence that makes ends and beginnings.

Another way in which ends and beginnings are seen in the sequence of our front reality is in the nature of cycles. If we travel the gestalt of *all that is* forwards, which we have named the way we face the world, we face the division of experience and constant choosing which creates the identity and prevents it from being dissipated. This choosing in any such pyramid structure leads to an accumulation of 'might-have-been' realities, because each possibility rejected has increasing possibilities of further choice but only one is chosen, and when that itself presents a choice only one is chosen again. Each time a multitude is ignored.

So one result of seeing reality as being relative is that we see our front reality having progressively less of our reality layer while our back reality contains relatively more. This is like saying that the more acutely we focus the more is left out of that focus. This process cannot continue indefinitely if front and back are both equally real as we are supposing; the balance of reality would logically become so one-sided that feelings of reality in the front would be restricted, narrow, unreal: we would expect there to be a transition to the opposite tide making back awareness more real again, magic returning and exact detail failing to support feelings of reality. In this way we would then travel the gestalt in the other direction towards what we call realization, or putting divisions together, which would produce the quite different experience of realizing completeness.

This cyclic nature of our reality is evident in all our activities and all that we observe, the cycle seeming to be one of the inescapable results of seeing *all that is* in sequence. Not only do all activities have this form but they occur at all frequencies; this same flow is seen as the expansion and contraction of universes, the rise and fall of civilizations, the formation and dissolution of societies, the growth and decay of plants and people, the year, month, week and day, or the vibration of molecules.

One interesting result of understanding cycles as being the sequential way of seeing *all that is* (our way) is that we can see also that if this sequence was the only way of seeing *all that is*, it would logically not have a cyclic nature but would be linear and endless. For the cyclic nature to appear we have to have a back reality and there has to be at least one other way of seeing *all that is* apart from division, choosing and sequence.

If we are to keep our thoughts clear when using the line language to image reality we always need to be definite about which frequency, what particular thread of activity, we are concerned with at any particular moment; the language describes *all that is* and equally it describes all views of *all that is*, however narrow, which are reality states. This can be confusing until one gets used to it.

To relate this cyclic nature to our present social experience, the world awareness of the twentieth century is rapidly sharing its consciousness and showing all the signs as a world unit of reaching the limits of travel towards front awareness. This is being felt as unreal, narrow and tense, but as we break down forms of rigid division to see both sides of all questions and release this tension, we find it difficult or impossible to accept the decay of structures by which we identify ourselves; these are social and moral as well as physical.

The trauma of this change involves fear of annihilation, a change of identity or ego-sense (personal and social) which is at present the way we experience the sequence of choice. As we cease to choose we feel our own identity crumble, and if we are convinced that we are this choosing ego we see our death. When such a change is possible we often choose instead some further refinement of choosing to avoid this trauma: when we do so, we put off our death and so cannot be reborn.

Without a change in our identification (what we believe we are) all transitions to wider experience of *all that is*, all salvations, are approached through a death, and history must follow this reality. Clinging to the structures of our civilization, we approach a new age through cataclysm.

So rebirth presupposes the death of a form; if we think we are that form it is we who die, for what survives does not have that form. Death then is a mirage of self-identification, and very convincing too.

THE LANGUAGE

One-line, two-line and three-line words

The flow which our own life force has between
our front and back realities is our own intimate
experience of the general pattern of cycles. As
we have immediate knowledge of what these
movements are like, we can recognize how the
binary lines of yin and yang combine in different ways to express them.

Back reality, the unmanifest depth, appears to
consciousness as potential activity or the store
from which activity comes, so for this we use
the ▬▬▬ (yang) symbol which is continuous
and so represents no change. The ▬▬ ▬▬ (yin)
symbol, on the other hand, is there in parts and
absent in parts and so presents us with change,
which is also activity. As we see this activity as
energy emerging from a stored state we understand the ▬▬▬ as the giver of activity and the
▬▬ ▬▬ as the receiver. Further, growth in our
world is what we call upwards, so we put these
factors together and make a statement of our
reality from the bottom ▬▬▬ to the top
▬▬ ▬▬ :

▬▬ ▬▬
▬▬▬▬

This is the first and most fundamental line
language statement about our reality. Considered carefully it implies everything I have said
so far; developed it will say everything I have to
say.

To develop a language out of these two
primary words we allow all the possible arrangements that these lines themselves possess to
represent what is possible, for what is possible is
reality. Firstly, a polarity can be seen either way
up, like an argument:

Seeing these from the bottom upwards, as our
reality tends to do in sequence, they are tending
to become:

These four two-line words are all the possible
arrangements of yin and yang in pairs.

Our primal statement ( ) speaks of
potential force and activity together embracing
reality. When seen from our sequential choosing
point of view there is a movement from one to
the other which has meaning for us. The four
states then become stages of a cyclic movement
(from the bottom):

4　　The state of potential

3　　From activity to the potential

2　　The state of activity

1　　From potential to activity

While these pairs express elements of change they do not include the flow that change involves. The idea of change or growth starts with one condition, has a transition, and ends with a new condition; so the idea has three elements, not two. To make a line word to express this flow we must include something of where we are going or where we have come from, so we add to any two-line word the beginning or end of any of the others to express change from one condition to the next. There are eight possible ways of doing this, which develop as follows:

When 1 is emerging from 4, activity is just about to emerge from the potential, so for this we draw ⚏ which is the I Ching trigram Tui.

When 1 begins to become 2 the potential becomes active and we draw ⚎ which is the trigram Chên.

There is activity alone as we move out of 1 through 2 and into 3, and this is the trigram ⚏ called K'un.

3 then emerges out of 2 and activity again seeks the potential, making ⚍ which is the trigram Kên.

When 3 is approaching 4 activity is being replaced by the inactive and what was fluid becomes solid; this makes the trigram ☴ called Sun.

Then there is the state of potentiality where all energy is undivided and inactive as 3 moves through 4 to 1 and we draw the trigram ☰ called Ch'ien.

There are two other states in this sequence which have to do with hesitation and fluctuation. When, in 3, activity is becoming potential it may not quite reach that state and revert towards 2, producing ☵ which is the trigram K'an. Conversely, 1 may not come fully into the active state before reverting to 4, producing ☲ the trigram Li. This reversion can equally be seen as a suppression of the extreme states Ch'ien and K'un, so that 3 becomes interlocked with 1 to produce either K'an or Li. In either way of expression there is a distrust of the definite, of commitment.

These eight trigrams are all the primary movements that can occur from the four states of pairs, which are themselves all the variants of the primary statement. Because they act out movements in life activity which we all experience we can recognize their outer effects, which are the meanings traditionally attached to the trigrams.

TUI

Tranquillity is nearly action.
Budding promises a spring.
Joy in the heart is quiet
yet quickening.
Thoughts the mind does not yet know.
The brim of the lake is overflowing.

CHÊN

Charge discharged.
Reality cracks.
Energy runs yin —
Claps whole again.
Relief is new normality.

K'UN

Growing is the joy of growing.
Damp earth feeds, seeds,
needs, receives the universe
in flowing life.
Becoming ever earth.

KÊN

Pressure of growth in limits
folds mountains, climbs,
slows momentum.
Views from above, beyond.
Knows new boundaries
where still horizons hold him.

SUN

Growing from fluid into firm
like wood grows strong but bends
in the wind maturing.
Bone.
Crystallizing lattice forms an image
of the end of growth.

15

CH'IEN

Of tranquillity, a being.
Harvested and not yet sown. Seed.
Home. Being without need
and source of needing.

K'AN

Yet we cannot leave.
We cannot rest.
We cannot choose
and are beset with doubt.
Knowing only narrowly
we must flow out
for here is danger, resting.

LI

Tentatively too we seek to fly
while clinging to the firm.
We shyly try, pretend.
The flame clings to the wood —
is gone again.

THE LANGUAGE

Four-line and five-line words

The line language expresses more of *all that is* as we add further lines to make longer line words. Each time we add another line we find a new group of line words with twice as many words in it as the group before it; thus there are 2 lines, 4 pairs, 8 trigrams, 16 quadragrams, 32 pentagrams, 64 hexagrams and so forth.

It is the 64 hexagrams which form the I Ching oracle because the hexagram represents the complete cycle of reality in which man finds himself. The two systems between the trigrams and the hexagrams, 16 quadragrams and 32 pentagrams, provide some information to tell us how this is so.

The primal statement ▬▬ speaks of the nature of each layer of reality being divided and whole; then the four states of that pair speak of the phases of a cyclic movement which is the nature of reality within the layer; the trigrams speak of the flow of change within the cycle which is how that reality is experienced. The meaning of each of these groups of line words builds up from the meaning of the groups of smaller line words within them.

We have seen how the trigram is made as we travel from one pair to another, so two pairs are always involved in the trigram, for example:

trigram → 2 pairs

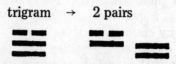

These two pairs are the only components of the trigram apart from its three lines, which already give it the character of change. The number two is symbolic of polarity and the pair speaks of a reality layer, so two pairs have the meaning of a reality layer seen as polarity. We choose amongst these polarities and so experience change, and the composite meaning of the trigram becomes 'change by choosing' which is also growth.

For all the groups of line words we derive symbolic meanings in this same way, so the sequence of understanding is kept both simple and logical as the meanings of the groups of line words grow naturally with the lines themselves.

Following this pattern the quadragram is found to have 3 pairs and 2 trigrams as well as its 4 lines:

quadragram → 3 pairs → 2 trigrams

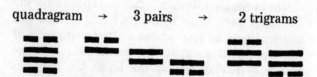

We understand three as change and the pair as a reality layer, so the three pairs speak of change of or in a reality layer. Because the three grammatically qualifies the pair we use the symbolic meaning of three to qualify the symbolic meaning of the pair, thus keeping the structure the same.

Then there are two trigrams which are symbolically a polarity (2) of or in the flow of change by choosing (trigram).

The quadragram is also four lines and the meaning that four has for us can be seen in the way this number has been used throughout our civilization. The completion of a cycle of our activity is our week of 7 days which is 3 (activity or change) with 4. What is necessary with activity to make a cycle is the decay of that activity, its completion. Another way we use four is in our expression of the most that a cycle achieves, which is the product of growth and decay: this is 3×4, or 12, which is the number of our ultimate types, or archetypes, the zodiac, tarot cards and apostles.

These two usages show that we understand four symbolically as completion and decay in a cycle. The number four is also directly linked to cycles in that every cycle has four different phases. Looked at as a rising and falling wave these are the rise, the crest, the fall and the trough; in breathing they are inhalation, tension, exhalation and relaxation; for the moon we have made this four weeks.

So the quadragram has to do with the whole of a cycle, its structure, and its completion and decay; this indicates that for us it is the whole we cannot have in consciousness and the decay we do not choose, the complement of growth in our cycles of growth and decay. To look at the component words again: the cycle we know is both change of and in a polarity layer (the quadragram's three pairs), while the polarity or direction of the flow of growth (two trigrams) is our experience of that cycle.

Our front reality gives us an ambivalent attitude to this character of four; it is the very personal one of our identity which we strive to complete but do not wish to decay. It takes much experience in duality before completion and decay can be seen as the same and identity as irrelevant.

The words within five-line words

The pentagram, having 5 lines, also contains groups of line words with less than 5 lines; 2 quadragrams, 3 trigrams, and 4 pairs, for example:

We already have some ideas for the symbolic meanings of lines, pairs, trigrams and quadragrams and also for the numbers 1, 2, 3 and 4, so we can put these meanings together in the combinations we find in the component words of the pentagram to discover what this is about. Firstly, though, the pentagram is five lines.

Apparently because of our five digits on each hand, which so clearly divide the ten between left and right, the number five has become the half-way mark of our cycle of counting in tens. The binary line system in which we are making images of reality counts in cycles of two, not of ten, and the half-way mark becomes also the step before the next completion. So because of our hands, which have been of basic importance in our development as man, five has a meaning of half which requires the other half to make a whole.

Now, if we look at the position of the five-line word amongst the other line words which make up the hexagram we see that the meanings of the others together express three of the four phases of a cycle.

The division of unity is expressed by the pair — this is a birth of activity. This division causes choice amongst polarity (direction) which is expressed by the trigram and produces identity. This direction becomes completed or exhausted and decayed, which is expressed by the quadragram. And the pentagram? To complete the cycle the pentagram would need to express a movement in the opposite direction to the growth by choosing of the trigrams and lead to transition opposite to the division of unity by the pairs. These are the meanings of its component line words.

The two quadragrams speak of the polarity of completion while the four pairs speak conversely of the completion of polarity: these are the opposite of division. The three trigrams talk of the change in the reality state of choosing, which opposes it to the state of choosing itself.

So the sum of the pentagram characteristics describes the phase we ourselves aspire to and find so difficult to achieve because it involves the end of the form we think of as ourselves; the pentagram stage is changing the identification we have with five, with half the polarity, to an identification with ten, the whole. So in the hexagram, the whole cycle, we next find two pentagrams.

THE LANGUAGE

The six-line word

The hexagram is of course one stage more complex than the pentagram; it contains 2 pentagrams, 3 quadragrams, 4 trigrams, 5 pairs, and its 6 lines, for example:

hexagram   2 pentagrams   3 quadragrams

4 trigrams   5 pairs

The two pentagrams speak of polarity (2) seeking union (pentagram); the three quadragrams speak of change (3) of completion/decay (quadragram); the four trigrams speak of the completion/decay (4) of change by choice (trigram); while the five pairs speak of seeking union (5) amongst polarity (pair).

These statements are two grammatical pairs, each pair looking at one aspect of the hexagram from front or back. Thus two pentagrams say there is a polarity of choosing while five pairs state that there is choosing amongst polarity.

The other aspect of the hexagram is expressed as three quadragrams which say there is a change in or towards the completion, or four trigrams which speak of the completion of change (as a mode of being).

The hexagram, then, is firstly about the choosing amongst polarities in our reality, and we have already seen that this choosing creates our state of change, our flow and our identity; this is then stated to come to completion/decay (the reality changes itself as 3 x 4 or 4 x 3 and both come to our 12 archetypes). So the hexagram represents a whole cycle; in this the pair group sets out into difference, the trigram group experiences this difference in sequence and direction, the quadragram group sees the completion and decay of that sequence for us, and the pentagram group sees the change in identity that leads to the completion of the cycle (the acceptance of the whole).

In all its aspects the hexagram pictures the complete cycle which is its primary meaning for us in the cycle of our own reality. We now focus on the four trigrams which represent the experience of our cyclic flow, the completion of change. It is these which form the oracle images and from these also comes the name I Ching, the book of changes; this refers to an aspect of *all that is* that is man's experience until this phase as man is ended by him changing his own identity.

So, approaching the oracle, we now pick out this aspect of the hexagram which describes our experience, the four trigrams which speak of the completion of change. When we arrive at this completion we have come to the archetypes in which we complete our world, but we are at present still accomplishing this, and the way in which we experience the cycles of our activity is in the four phases of changing states which are the four trigrams; it is these, speaking from our point of view, which form the images for an oracle of our present reality. After our completion the hexagram images and oracle will no longer describe our reality.

In the hexagram these images are interwoven as trigrams:

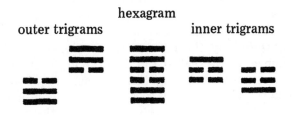

hexagram

outer trigrams   inner trigrams

Each trigram expresses either a state of change between yin and yang or their extremes, so the hexagram is able to express the four changes that appear in all complete cycles. Relating these to our own life flow, as we read the flow of line words from the bottom upwards the bottom trigram has to do with the way we begin or prepare our activity (this is before we are conscious of our intentions), the middle two are concerned with the way we perform these intentions and how we react to what happens, and the top trigram of the hexagram is about how we accept or reject the experience in which we are involved. This is our basic cycle as described by the hexagram components.

Activity appears from somewhere in our obscure depths as something like a need — a need for experience of a certain kind, which is at first a vague feeling. This becomes more definite and focused as a polarity towards this and away from that. We then act out this feeling in our lives. The cycle continues as we reabsorb the meaning that experience has for us, arranging our attitudes and saying we have gained experience. The different ways there are of doing this are described by the flow of changes in the hexagrams.

The choosing that we do continually is expressed by the lines of the hexagram which change, as we shall see in detail later. There are two results of having this choosing sequential reality. One we have seen to be the continual subdivision of reality into complexity; the other is that whenever we are between any two poles, when one is achieved the other becomes desirable. This is inevitably part of a cyclic reality such as we have seen pictured in the hexagram.

We can distinguish two modes in our choosing, however, which can be roughly compared with circles and cycles. The difference between these is that one repeats while the other goes through a transition to another layer or dimension where it repeats the basic cycle but in quite a new way. We do both of these things in a complex pattern where they are too interdependent to distinguish entirely, but we all recognize the repetition of situations where we have chosen to re-experience rather than change our own identity in that situation, which would complete its cycle. When we do change this part of our identity we experience a realization, and all the changes which make up our growth or evolution are punctuated with these, great or small; they are the quanta in which our experience of *all that is* expands.

MAKING HEXAGRAMS

We have been looking at ideas which reflect an embracing view of *all that is* in which we find ourselves. When we now approach the oracle in practice we limit ourselves to the part of this organization which is immediately relevant to us and a part of that which is active at a given moment. This is what casting hexagrams is about. The six-line words reflect our own reality, and we have just seen how these relate to us amongst the more general pattern.

The sixty-four hexagrams are not an approximation of all the states we can get into; they are nearer to being the musical intervals, the notes we commonly use to divide the octave of our experience, and we play these as chords as well as melodies. The oracle has to distinguish which part of the melody is being played and which notes of its chords belong to a particular question. The melody goes on continually, but the hexagram is an arrested moment of it and would be quite unreal in this stillness if the language did not allow for the fact that the pattern is continually changing. It does this in the same way that it developed in the first place, by allowing the lines to move from all possible arrangements to all other possible arrangements, nothing being selected and nothing left out; there are 4096 of these and the oracle has this number of different responses.

When one hexagram turns into another by changing lines, some of the lines may be the same as before and some will have changed from yang to yin or yin to yang. Those which change are known as moving lines.

Now, because this language represents a flow pattern this changing of lines is not a binary action like the flick of a switch, yang or yin; it is a cyclic flow which is yinwards or yangwards like a tide, although we only express it as yang or yin. There is a mechanism in the methods of casting hexagrams which decides at what point the change is considered to have occurred. This is most clear in the yarrow stalk method which we shall look at in detail in a minute.

We have next to consider what happens when a hexagram is cast. This process selects one of the 4096 arrangements of words which gives insight into the question in the mind of the enquirer. This is a 'magical' part of the oracle because only one end of what happens is in our front reality and we cannot experience any other aspect of reality in consciousness. Because of this we will not attempt here to form more detailed concepts about the way magic operates, knowing that whatever image we may now make will of necessity be greatly distorted.

Hexagrams are cast by one of several processes which involve what we call chance, and in practice this means that we arrange not to choose the outcome consciously. To cast hexagrams we either throw three similar coins like dice and note the combinations of the upper faces, which we then assess, or we divide a pile of forty-nine stalks into two at random and then sort the resulting piles in a specially symbolic way.

These are not the only ways in which it can be done; any choice from which consciousness is excluded is influenced by the back reality of the chooser. Conscious choices are partly influenced in this way as well, but because reality outside consciousness is seen as non-real these effects are largely ignored. There is a basic sense in which *all* our experience is chosen and indivisible once the identification of who is choosing is widened.

There are, then, these two ways of casting hexagrams in common use. Both produce six lines, each yin or yang, and both methods have a built-in mechanism which decides at what point of balance we call their movement yin or yang. That there is a point of balance means that there are two states where we have a foot in each category while moving from one to the other, yang to yin or yin to yang; these are allowed for in both casting methods, being known as moving lines. The change from yang to yin is thought of as an old yang line becoming a young yin line and is written ▬O▬ . The opposite movement is an old yin line becoming a young yang line and is written ▬X▬ .

Here are the two ways of casting a hexagram.

The coin method

Take three coins of the same sort and decide that one face is yang and the other yin. Having made this choice, always keep it the same.

For each line of the hexagram, starting with the bottom line, all three coins are thrown together like dice and the upper faces noted. Thus they are thrown six times altogether, and for each throw the faces will have one of the following combinations:

combination of faces	written symbol
A majority of yin faces (young yang line)	▬▬▬
A majority of yang faces (young yin line)	▬▬ ▬▬
All three yang faces (old yang line)	▬O▬
All three yin faces (old yin line)	▬X▬

The symbols for the throws are then written in a pile, the first one cast being put at the bottom, for instance:

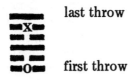

last throw

first throw

The yarrow stalk method

Fifty thin straight sticks are needed, thin enough for the bunch to be held comfortably in one hand and thick enough to allow them to be handled easily one at a time. A convenient length is between a hand and a foot length. The sticks need not be yarrow stalks but should be something you like to handle.

One stalk is laid aside for the whole time, then:

1. The remaining forty-nine stalks are laid down and divided. After aiming at the middle of the pile with the thumb of the right hand the two piles are separated.
2. One stalk is taken from the right-hand pile and is held between the third and little fingers of the left hand.
3. Each pile is counted off in groups of four stalks until four or less of each pile remain.
4. These two remainders, each four or less, are put together with the one held by the little left-hand finger in a separate pile. There will be five or nine stalks.
5. The other stalks are gathered together and operations 1 to 4 are repeated. This time the separate pile will have four or eight stalks.
6. Operation 5 is repeated once more.

There are now three piles of stalks set aside and in these piles there are 5 or 9 stalks, 4 or 8 stalks, and 4 or 8 stalks. Each pile contains either a large number of stalks (9 or 8) or a small number (5 or 4). The combinations of large and small numbers in the three piles decide the nature of the line.

combination	written symbol
2 large + 1 small (e.g. 9.4.8.) is a young yang line	▬▬▬
1 large + 2 small (e.g. 5.8.4.) is a young yin line.	▬▬ ▬▬

3 large numbers (9.8.8.)
is an old yin line.

■X■

3 small numbers (5.4.4.)
is an old yang line.

■O■

7. The appropriate symbol from these is written down as the bottom line of the hexagram.
8. Actions 1 to 7 are repeated for each line of the hexagram.

This may seem a long process, but with familiarity it only takes five or six minutes.

Using either of these methods you now have a hexagram with or without moving lines. If there are none you have a simple hexagram, for instance:

The two outer trigrams of these are upper ☱ Tui and lower ☳ Chên. Using the key at the back of the book, find the hexagram number corresponding to these upper and lower trigrams (in this case 17). Then find this numbered hexagram in the oracle and read this only; the moving line comments on the left do not apply.

If, however, there are one or more moving lines the oracle is carried in three separate parts.

For example, if you cast

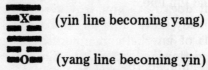

(yin line becoming yang)

(yang line becoming yin)

first write the hexagram in its 'old' form,

then note down which lines have moved, in this case the bottom and fifth.

Now write the hexagram in its 'new' form with the moving lines changed into their opposites.

After finding both the hexagrams from the key read the page of the first hexagram completely, then the moving line comments for the lines that have moved in your hexagram only; the others do not apply. Then read the page for the second hexagram completely, but do not read any of the moving lines for this.

This, then, is the information that the oracle can give you. The form in which I have written it this time will be explained a little later. The information is the same whichever method of casting we use, but the way in which we respond to the answers is not necessarily the same. The reader, by selecting a particular arrangement of words, is trying to tell his consciousness some things it does not know together with things it does already know. For this to be successful his channels of internal communication need to be open and flowing, and for this the yarrow stalk ritual was most beautifully devised.

The coin method of casting is very simple and quick and produces as true a hexagram as the yarrow stalk method — as we have seen, the mechanism is the same. We do not, however, spend much time with ourselves, and in throwing the coins we tend to externalize our query in symbolism so that the answer comes back to us as though the book of hexagram images was itself speaking. Reflections of our inner knowing are in the hexagram images and line movements, and the rich symbolism of the yarrow stalk ritual uses our inner channels where this relationship flows.

It is for this reason that the ritual is to be more recommended. It was designed with great caring and its movements release internal tensions through the inner flow it creates, linking the greater being. Many times there is a knot in one's life which is no longer there after this ritual, even when no specific conscious solution appears.

Our use of this ritual will be nourished if we have some conscious image of what it is about. It starts with the removal of one of the fifty stalks; this one is a recognition of that aspect of the cycle of growth and decay which does not take part in these activities, the potential or undivided one. This stalk is not used as we are enquiring about the flow, not its source.

The original number of stalks, fifty, is the sum of the number symbols which the line language produces to express growth. The language produces another flow of number symbols to express decay, and the sum of these is also fifty. The completion of the cycle of growth and decay is then one hundred (one is seen symbolically as being complete and we count in cycles of ten). These symbol structures of growth and decay lead into rather lengthy and abstract views which are not particularly relevant to the oracle. Here it may be noticed that the sum of the components of the hexagram are:

6 lines	= 6
5 pairs	= 10
4 trigrams	= 12
3 quadragrams	= 12
2 pentagrams	= 10
	50 lines

The pattern of flow that we seek amongst growth and decay is always present between our outer and inner levels; when we divide the pile of forty-nine stalks into two parts we can tell the state of this tide from the position of the division: towards yang, towards yin, or in transition. We look for this trend consecutively up the hexagram for each line of our flow pattern.

After each division of the stalks into two we take one stalk from the right-hand pile and hold it, in abeyance as it were, by the little finger of the left hand. This transfer of something from right to left is symbolic of a message from outer to inner, but it is also more than this: every time action takes place in the world we divide the potential and active, as we have just done with the stalks, and to maintain a whole view of what we are — that these divided realities are images of each other — a sacrifice is made, a link from acute consciousness to acknowledge the presence of ourselves. Without this link the harmony of action is lost.*

It is interesting to note that in terms of our technology this link is feedback, without which no self-regulating system can operate.

When we have made this symbolic recognition that our nature is whole we divide the two piles of stalks into groups of four to see what remains incomplete after our choice. In the final or remaining group of each pile there may be 1, 2, 3 or 4 stalks, and as we make the division three times for each line the possible remainders from our choice are:

	left pile	held	right pile		left pile	held	right pile
1st choice	4 +	1 +	4 = 9	or	1 +	1 +	3 = 5
				or	2 +	1 +	2 = 5
				or	3 +	1 +	1 = 5
2nd and 3rd	4 +	1 +	3 = 8	or	2 +	1 +	1 = 4
choice	or 3 +	1 +	4 = 8	or	1 +	1 +	2 = 4

In this table it can be seen that the difference between choices which result in a large number (9 or 8) and a small number (5 or 4) is that to produce 9 or 8 a complete group of 4 stalks

---

* Roger Maybank, with his usual symbolic acumen, has pointed out to me that yarrow's latin name is achillea and that in legend Achilles was taught by the centaur Cheiron to use yarrow for the healing of sword wounds. As the sword divides so the yarrow makes whole; as the activity in front reality divides so the yarrow stalk ritual heals this wound in our being.

remains on either the left- or right-hand pile, while to get 4 or 5 there are no groups of 4 stalks on either pile.

This is the mechanism which decides yang or yin in the flow. When we have a majority of large numbers from our three divisions we produce a yang (▬▬) line, and a majority of small numbers produces a yin (▬ ▬) line, so each choice, each division of the stalks, gives a leaning of the line towards yin or yang chosen by the four symbolism distinguishing between completeness (potential action) and incompleteness demanding action. The majority of the three choices determines whether the tide of the line is yin or yang, or in transition because it has reached an extreme of yin or yang (5.4.4. or 9.8.8.).

So the yarrow stalk method selects yang or yin from the point of view of the four symbolism, while the coin method is only concerned with the three symbolism. This results in a difference of notation; the majority of coin faces chosen as yang makes a young yin line whereas a majority of yang tendencies in the yarrow stalk method results in a young yang line. This difference neatly compensates the effect of looking at the symbolism from front or back reality. Looked at from the outside a pressure of potential is seen as activity coming, while seen from inside it is more simply a state of being.

It may also be noticed that the first choice in dividing the stalks has three times as many active chances as potential ones, reflecting our choice of growth as desirable and decay as the unlovely one. In the coin method the chances of throwing yin and yang are equal; being approached from the front reality the bias is already included in our attitude.

There is a slightly shorter version of the yarrow stalk ritual which does not lose much in symbolic meaning. When the left-hand pile has been divided off into fours the remainder of the right-hand pile is a foregone conclusion, so we need not count these as well. This method is accomplished as follows:

1. Take the fifty stalks and put one aside.
2. Place the forty-nine stalks before you and divide at random with the right thumb into two piles.
3. Take one from the right-hand pile and hold it with the little finger of the left hand.
4. Count off the left-hand pile only in groups of four stalks.
5. Add to the remainder of this left-hand pile (four or less) the stalk in your left hand.
6. If the remainder is now 4 or less make it up to 5 from the right-hand pile. If it is 5 make it up to 9. Put these (5 or 9) aside.
7. Gather the remaining stalks and divide again into two piles; repeat operations 3, 4 and 5.
8. If the remainder is now 2 or 3 make it up to 4; if it is 4 or 5 make it up to 8. Set these aside also.
9. Repeat 7 and 8 to produce three piles of stalks. The result is written down in the same way as for the full-length method (page 31).

THE ORACLE IMAGES AND MOVING LINES

We now have some understanding of the line language as a picture of relativity arranging itself to form layers of reality. This has led us to look at a layer of meaning that is one wider than the polarities in our conscious world in order to have a model of the forces underlying our activity. By associating this understanding with pairs of lines and allowing these to grow into trigrams we found images of situations we may be involved with. Then by placing one trigram upon another we expressed these situations in the cyclic nature of our experience, using the four trigrams of a hexagram. The casting of a hexagram we then saw as an arrested moment of this constantly flowing experience.

The images which we read in the oracle for each hexagram are composed from the mutual influence of these four trigrams, and when the trigrams and their meanings are read at the top of the page of hexagram images this logical thread of the oracle can be followed if we wish.

The images for each hexagram are expressed in four forms labelled pattern, nature, human and form. The pattern brings out the relationships the trigrams have together, each contributing to this from its particular position in the hexagram. This pattern corresponds to a natural condition which is labelled nature. The human experience of this takes account of our particularly motivated direction in such a pattern and so is labelled human. The label 'form' announces the social and other externalized forms by which we recognize such patterns.

These images are also a way of expressing the four phases of experience in a way we can see as structure, not as sequence.

The origin of the comments on the moving lines needs some further explanation and involves seeing the hexagrams in a slightly different way. The line language sees everything from back and front. We have just seen the hexagram as an image looking out on the world. In the moving lines we turn to view ourselves.

When a hexagram is cast all the lines may have simple flows yinwards or yangwards; this produces a single hexagram for which we read all the appropriate hexagram images only and no moving lines because nothing has moved. Alternatively we may find some lines in transition, producing the three-part answer composed as follows:

1. The images for the hexagram made by using the 'old' form of the moving lines.
2. The comments on the lines that have moved in this hexagram.
3. The images for the hexagram made using the 'young' form of the moving lines (ignoring the moving line comments for this hexagram).

These three parts indicate change in the flow of experience because three is the nature of change and transition is its middle term. This transition is brought about by our changing our choice of experience, and also part of our identity, so the moving line is a reaction of the psyche to the situation pictured in the first hexagram (the old form).

The hexagram pattern grows from the bottom upwards and as it does so our internal activity, expressed by the bottom lines, comes out into conscious activity in the middle lines and is then absorbed again as 'experience' in the top lines.

We have already seen that choosing amongst reality is a matter of either focusing on a part which makes it active or conscious, or ignoring it which removes it from conscious experience. This is matched in the line language by ▬ ▬ for activity and ▬▬ for the inactive.

So putting these factors together, each line of the hexagram refers to a level of the psyche, and its state of yin or yang tells whether that level is actively choosing (changing) or not.

These levels are only labels of convenience referring to functions of the psyche. We are expressing them as layers of our reality because this is how we tend to feel them. Here they are described in the order in which they are found in each group of moving line commentaries on the left-hand hexagram pages:

Bottom line	This is a layer in which we prepare our inner needs. It is beneath consciousness and here reality is less individual, more shared.

Second line	This is a layer of feeling where the essence is turned into the particular. The many ways in which a need for experience can be given form are here sorted out, feeling and emotion determining the way we experience things.
Third line	Here is conscious ego-self activity where particular experience can be felt acutely because awareness is in a narrow focus.
Fourth line	We select what we need to be real about our ego-self activity, and choose what ignorance we need to have about outside experience. This positions our focus and so regulates the ego activity of line three.
Fifth line	This expresses how we choose our feelings about our incoming experience. We re-turn the particular into our essence, taking notice of some and ignoring others, which sets the pattern of our choice in line two.
Top line	We react to the overall reality pattern of the moment, accepting it into ourselves or ignoring it. Here we constantly choose our inner reality and so the needs we next co-ordinate in line one.

As we travel from the bottom line of the hexagram to the top there is a breathing outwards to our conscious world in the middle of the hexagram and an inhaling of experience as we approach the top. This forms a cyclic flow between our inner and outer worlds, and it is the way this flow operates in an existing pattern expressed by the hexagram images that determines our experience. When we have a method of distinguishing this flow, which we have in the magical part of the oracle procedure, we can then choose our experience from the needs of our more whole being. It is important to realize that this 'more whole' being is not our whole being: *all that is* is the only whole being and so is also our whole being.

Changes can be accomplished with little effort at one time which at other times would be impossible. It is part of the operation of the oracle to help us distinguish between these. Consider for a moment a being who identifies himself with 'shut' and who has a longing for 'open'; then when he reaches 'open' he is scared and longs for 'shut'. For a long time he may swing between these two poles, longing for the one he is not expressing at the moment, but there are times in his cycle where it is possible to make the choice of seeing the whole polarity of 'shut-open' which removes him from that cycle altogether into a new realization, in this case the control of flow. It is only possible to do this at a point of balance where the two are experienced together, and this occurs when he has gone through the cycle enough times so that its separate realities are exhausted for him.

All our experience operates in these cycles, and the oracle is able to distinguish these moments and so make our activities more harmonious and our cycles less protracted.

The line language itself makes no moral judgements. These are the guiding feelings which come from a particular viewpoint or reality layer and they always balance the outer reality, never coinciding with it. Recognized or not they are always part of a reality layer, coming from that part of it which is not in focus or conscious. As the line language expresses both halves of everything it has no judgement to make.

When an oracle is made, however, two things are expected; one is that guidance will be given for outer activity and the other is that greater integration shall come to its user. To guide consciousness it is necessary to have something in the nature of a moral judgement or a direction in which it is best to go, and this judgement has to exactly fit the balance of the moment. This seeks the need of that person at that time, and has nothing to do with fixed goals such as goodness or bliss which are seen as always relative.

It is only by using the oracle that its presence can be experienced, and the effect that this experience gradually has upon our ability to expand into ourselves is the gift that some intelligence offers us from a time before our history began — and offers to us now. Writing the commentaries in a new form tries to bring us nearer to that intelligence, it does not try to encompass it with our logic. The logic is there to show our own intelligence the limitations of its sequence and the sequence of its limitations. The foot may be divided in the mind into twelve inches (archetypes) but it is the foot we walk upon; even as yet a polarity of feet.

What follows is the internal oracle and is complementary to the existing Chinese oracle and its translations. Principally it is the oracle of the yarrow stalks and as it is used our reality is seen from the inside, from the depth. Many questions of an external nature will be more clearly answered by the Chinese symbolisms which were assembled for the growth period; this present oracle is designed for the completion period of our time and some generations hence as the depth becomes more real.

SUMMARIZED NOTES ON THE USE OF THE ORACLE

A diagram for finding the number of any hexagram from its upper and lower trigrams is at the end of this book.

If you cast a hexagram with no moving lines read only the hexagram images for that hexagram, not any moving lines.

If you cast a hexagram with moving lines:
1. Make the hexagram with the lines in their 'old' form.
2. Note down which lines have moved.
3. Make the hexagram with the lines in their 'young' form.

Read the hexagram images for 1 and the

moving line comments for the lines that have moved. Read also the hexagram images for 3 but not any of the moving lines for this hexagram. (For fuller instructions see pages 32—4.)

Throughout the oracle text the person for whom the oracle is cast is referred to as 'he'. Usually this is the enquirer herself — or himself.

Moving line comments picture choices in the situation presented by their hexagram, so they all belong to the reality of someone who casts the hexagram. Only those which move in the hexagram refer to his outer life; the others belong to his back reality. Knowing this clearly he may gain clarity by reading them all, picking out those which have moved as belonging to his front reality. They are read from the bottom line to the top, and `to make this flow easier the bottom line is placed at the top of the page. Until you feel clear about separating these it is best to read only the lines that move.

**The simple only reappears
when the complex is exhausted**

PART TWO

The Hexagrams

1 Moving lines.

Responses to creative potential.

Bottom line   It is not yet time for action.
Preparation is being made.

Second line   Include as many viewpoints as possible.
Action while co-ordinating feeling
needs this balancing guidance.

Third line   There is plenty of time.
The feeling of overburden comes from
a large potential finding expression
in a narrow reality.

Fourth line   Being in the world is not being of it.
Being engrossed in outside activity uses
experience to the full. It is harmonious
to remember who is experiencing.

Fifth line   Balance feeling with the meaning of feeling.
If weaving feeling into a reality becomes
exclusive, there is less awareness.

Top line   Climb down where up has seemed best.
Climbing up a reflection is to go
further from its reality.

All trigrams are Ch'ien, in which
we see no movement.

Without it there can be no
movement.

1

Pattern   The creative power is ready.
           Awaits your sympathy
           like a new page.

Nature   The sun warms the earth.
           What will grow?
           Everything there is to flow
           and overflow.

Human   His decision, what form evolves.
           He is the king,
           head of his household.
           The world awaits the karma
           which is his endowment.

Form   The form is not yet.
           Riches are liquid, uncrystallized.
           The state has power.
           Its will is to be something.

2 Moving lines.

Choices amongst activity.

Bottom line   Fewer preparations lead to less activity.

Second line   Less co-ordination of feelings brings him
               nearer their source, and more direct
               expression serves him well.

Third line   Others can be assisted.
               Personal drive has slackened
               while activity remains.

Fourth line   There is less intimate experience of the
               world when reality is not in his personal
               activity.

Fifth line   When reality is not composed of feeling;
               active feelings beneath consciousness
               nevertheless bring wholeness to activity.

Top line   In a situation of activity he is passive,
               so there is conflict.

All trigrams are K'un, which
receives without choice and in
doing so gives without desire.

2

Pattern

Simple flow of activity.
Unquestioning.
Moves unjudged
accepting all things.

Nature

Onto the earth
warm and chill.
Into the earth
seed, root, love
moving in the magic of water.

Human

Born from the earth
of its elements.
Return sometimes unprotesting,
resting in the flowing juice of life.

Form

The only form he can make
is an empty tube.
The only government,
the will of the people.

3 Moving lines.

Difficulties in beginnings.

Bottom line   Seek strength and help to prepare activity
               at this time. Weak efforts are not enough.

Second line   His feelings are not yet ready for this
               challenge so he is deprived of driving power.
               Waiting for his feelings to become strong,
               then they will accept.

Third line   Acting out of the ego-self in times of
               difficulty due to ignorance would court
               failure, so he refrains from action.

Fourth line   Being unable to cope with difficulties alone
               halts him. When he can find other strength
               to join with, he can work through them.

Fifth line   He feels difficulties as part of beginnings.
               Such transitory difficulties due to inexperience
               are overcome by persistence. Persisting
               in continual difficulty dulls experience.

Top line   Driving power is developed by overcoming
               obstacles. He is not accepting this and
               becomes sorry for his own weakness.

Trigrams: Chên, K'un, Kên, K'an.
The creative bursts into the active
in Chên, fructifies the earth in
K'un, moves steeply towards a
standstill in Kên, and tries to flow
again in K'an.

Pattern

When the young flows first with
little stamina,
it is overcome by obstacles.
By flowing on it overcomes them.

Nature

Young growths grow fast, sappy,
and easily hurt against obstacles;
but new shoots are ready
to follow up.

Human

New things begin to move.
Difficulties arise in the path.
To halt at difficulty
brings out danger.
To persevere
brings on flowing.

Form

When first they come together
there is a honeymoon,
then a strength of will,
then a compromise
for the sake of travelling on together.

4 ▬▬ Moving lines.

Out of young ignorance.

Bottom line   Ignorance becomes established if it is not
               allowed to show. He can only learn to
               control experience by having it.

Second line   Open to the feeling of expression, ignorance
               soon becomes experience. He can have faith
               that in this freedom he will be fulfilled.

Third line   He was acting out in the glamour of his ego-self.
               Seeing himself, he desists, losing his freedom
               of movement.

Fourth line   Without recognizing himself as ignorant
               he cannot become otherwise.

Fifth line   Not feeling his ignorance as himself
               he can openly move into knowing.
               He does not become entangled in ignorance.

Top line   Accepting that knowing comes with experience
               it remains to make the movement neither
               too strong nor too weak.

Trigrams: K'an, Chên, K'un, Kên.
Growth (Chên) out of the water
(K'an) is the very beginning of
life. Out of water into earth
(K'un), out of earth up the
mountain (Kên) is a path of much
travelling.

Pattern   To reach from the fluid and unstable
                 for the heights
                 comes to a barrier,
                 or perhaps a peak.

Nature   Kittens catch shadows
                 knowing their solidity,
                 and learn.

Human   Assuming ground beneath the feet.
                 Treading with confidence into pitfalls,
                 sometimes succeeds
                 with a grace and sympathy
                 it usually lacks.

Form   Assumption of power
                 without humility
                 closes the gate of sympathy.

5   Moving lines.

Lack of a path.

Bottom line   Here paths originate. Continued
activity makes a way.

Second line   His feelings come and go as he tries
many ways. Others may not understand
this until he finds a way leading on.

Third line   He creates his own path, a circle of worry.

Fourth line   When he does not accept the absence of
life flow, he cannot recognize its reappearance.

Fifth line   Feeling the absence of a way forward
nourishes his awareness. When that
feeling changes he will know how to act.

Top line   Activity is artificial, without flow.
Not meeting the challenge of no track.
Watching for changes and getting involved
in these when they come brings on the flow.

Trigrams: Ch'ien, Tui, Li, K'an.
Slow to move into activity by
feeling the way coming (Ch'ien,
Tui). Tentatively active (Li) and
back and forth (K'an following Li).

Pattern From tranquil to fluid without course.
      Intimations desired action.
      No channel to guide a flow.

Nature   There is no track.

Human   Mood for action
      slowly stirred
      finds no path.
      Danger of floundering,
      do not run, swim gently.

Form   The wise do not listen
      to the cries of their opponents.
      Quench them with silence.

6 Moving lines.

Conflicting opposites.

Bottom line	Not preparing further action in conflict. He is using strength which will appear as weakness, but eventually it is recognized.
Second line	Seeing both sides, co-ordinating his feelings in a conflict. Changes from one extreme to another are balanced out.
Third line	Continuing to abstain from acting out the ego-self. Choosing other people's ends and also their means avoids entangling conflict.
Fourth line	He accepts the path as it is, obstructed, and no longer battles along it. Conflict occurs only in narrow realities, he may broaden his.
Fifth line	Conflict in his feelings. Accepting this he reasons out both sides and sees himself more clearly.
Top line	Conflict in his situation. Remaining in conflict, trying for one side to quell the other, has only fluctuating security. Winning and losing are both narrow realities.

Trigrams: K'an, Li, Sun, Ch'ien.   6
At the base are opposites and
uncertainty of position (K'an, Li),
becoming firm and aloof (Sun,
Ch'ien).

Pattern
:   Alternate water fire
    cannot grow together.
    Opposing into firmness
    is tranquillity of solitude.

Nature
:   Heat frustrates life functions of water,
    water, the cleansing of fire.
    When nature throws these together
    life takes time to recover.

Human
:   Conflict resolved by separation.
    Internal conflict, by distinctions.

Form
:   When an entity moves
    in opposing directions
    they each have need
    of a single sphere.

7   **≡≡**   Moving lines.

Many forms within one.

Bottom line   Before organizing experience it is
necessary to have clear needs. Unclear
needs lead to chaotic experience.

Second line   Harmonious change comes from co-ordinating
his feelings. This creates a many-sided
activity from his many needs.

Third line   Many-sided action is needed. He is not
using his ego-self to channel this.
Perhaps it is busy with activity that
has lost its meaning.

Fourth line   He can gain co-ordination without being
ruled by the ego-self. Though that is the
first way of advance he does not now accept it.

Fifth line   Without tackling real feelings experience
is deadened. Too many checks and balances
lead to no movement. Yet he does not
allow his flow of feeling to carry the life.

Top line   He builds a world.
He does this because he does not experience his
inner reality in detail, only in general.
Making an outside world with his life force
he reflects himself, but should not fall into
his reflection.

Trigrams: K'an, Chên, K'un, K'un.
Restless and fluid (K'an) releasing
activity (Chên) throughout the
earth (K'un, K'un).

Pattern

An appearance everywhere
of activity without rest.
A rising
or collecting together.
Many effects
with a single cause.

Nature

Water the earth
and out of every crevice
growth comes.

Human

Pervaded by one motivation
all fields of our activity
take their form.

Form

From a single control
the mass obeys.

8   Moving lines.

The Diverse.

Bottom line — He will prepare new experience later, at present he is full of elements he is weaving together.

Second line — Diversity of feelings does not allow co-ordination into action. The challenge remains and he does have the power, given time.

Third line — His environment does not complement his needs. Inner and outer experiences are diverse so one cannot flow into the other.

Fourth line — Accepting the sum of diversity is necessary for unity.

Fifth line — He does not rationalize the diversity of his feelings. Their changing flow nourishes him without this linear language.

Top line — His balance is upset because he does not accept the whole diverse field in his view.

Trigrams: K'un, K'un, Kên, K'an.
Activity in the earth (K'un, K'un)
makes a mountain (Kên) and an
abyss (K'an). 8

Pattern   Activity from the indivisible one
becomes high and low,
the still and the flowing.

Nature   A mountain rises from the land,
beyond is water in the deep.

Human   Where we are diverse
we have need
to complement one another.
Where we need to overcome an obstacle
we co-operate.
When divided in ourselves
we need to ask for guidance.

Form   He who sits on high
is able to see land and water
and provide what is lacking
from one to another.

9 Moving lines.

Using what is small.

Bottom line   Activity of his world will increase.
               He is preparing for this.

Second line   His driving power will increase.
               He is drawing his feelings together.

Third line   Even those in sympathy are antagonistic
               when he forces a pace he cannot support.
               He acts out of his ego-self with too
               little reserve.

Fourth line   He will gain from leaving it if he
               knows its narrowness.
               He is less active in his ego-self.

Fifth line   If he feels an urge to expand his
               awareness he will be nourished by
               his environment.

Top line   He can simply rejoice in this portent.
               He glimpses inner and outer, though he
               cannot maintain it.
               Trying to feel it more strongly he will
               lose its dual reality.

Trigrams: Ch'ien, Tui, Li, Sun.
Potential (Ch'ien) promises action
(Tui). This clings to the tranquil
(Li), quickly ripening (Sun).

9

Pattern

Creative tranquillity
feels for activity.
Hesitates to move.
A little movement
soon matures.

Nature

The sun breaks from the clouds
late in the day,
giving a mellow evening.
If a small fire is blown
it is soon ashes.

Human

To expect more than there is
will lose the value
of what we have.
To savour this little
gives nourishment.

Form

Wise government
and good craftsmen
attend to quality.

10 Moving lines.

Becoming real.

Bottom line The natural flow into physical reality.
He prepares his need for expression as
part of a general need.

Second line When feeling becomes real, form becomes
shadow, the divisions of form give way
to continuity of feeling. This intuitive
approach widens his awareness.

Third line The warrior makes himself not know.
Intentional ignorance allows him extraordinary
experience in danger, but if his ignorance
is real he learns by mistakes.

Fourth line Focusing his conscious eyes loses inner
sight (insight); this involves mistakes,
which are the way out of ignorance if he
is not reckless.

Fifth line Feeling becomes real. In the extreme it
overcomes and he is confused. He cannot
co-ordinate in any one facet of his reality.
Balance brings harmony.

Top line He looks for what is carrying his life flow,
for what is real. As he uncovers more of this
he mistakes less. The cover is made of
his actions.

Trigrams: Tui, Li, Sun, Ch'ien.
An inner glimpse (life force at the
surface) (Tui) acts briefly (Li),
becoming firm (Sun) in the
tranquil (Ch'ien).

10

Pattern
Life force shines through,
linking the outer with the inner.

Nature
The fire of heaven
draws the water in the earth.

Human
A knowing of inner knowing
gives a realization.
Making this firm in ourselves
increases potential.
Each realization takes a liberty
with the reality of the one,
but is also a link with it.

Form
To enter where power is
can easily be confused
with being that power.
To enter gently is not dangerous.

11 Moving lines.

Harmonious action.

Bottom line — The sun calls out the sun worshippers.
Action in the simple is inner need or
potential activity. It calls forth
the action of that need, action in the easy.

Second line — There are many ways open.
Treading many paths at each moment,
without forgetting himself, he will benefit.

Third line — Out of the simple, into the complex of the
ego-self; he may lose sight of himself.
Seek the simple that is still there in
the complex.

Fourth line — Allowing wealth to fade because it is no
longer real. The states of being are real
to him, not what they possess. Harmonious
in or out of action.

Fifth line — Creative development follows from feeling in
thought, neither of them laying claim to what
is real. Together they enact harmonious spirals.

Top line — Do not act on present assumptions. Greater
realities are unformed, but without them
formed realities collapse.

Trigrams: Ch'ien, Tui, Chên, K'un.
The potential life force (Ch'ien)
breaks into activity (Tui, Chên) in
the earth (K'un).

11

Pattern   Harmonious flow
               from the inner to the outer
               is power in the easy.

Nature   Unfolding the life force
               of the seed.

Human   Unimpeded movement.
               The path suits the traveller
               and he shines within.

Form   Form creates itself.
               Now we can see it.
               Shall we remember it
               when we desire?

12 Moving lines.

Standstill.

Bottom line   One does not come without the other.
Inaction of the inner need is stagnation
of activity.

Second line   Amongst many possibilities he holds back.
Others may take advantage but this control
strengthens him.

Third line   Why does he not act, they say.
He knows the road leads nowhere, and waits.

Fourth line   He keeps to his wholeness, accepting
inaction as part of activity.

Fifth line   Watching in peace needs strength. Opening
his mind to ways out of stagnation he
sees signs and nurtures them.

Top line   Standstill comes to an end when he
recognizes his inner needs. From these
he develops driving power for movement.

Trigrams: K'un, Kên, Sun, Ch'ien.
A mountain (Kên) stands between
earth activity (K'un) and its
ripening (Sun) into the tranquil
(Ch'ien).

 12

Pattern	Separation between the potential and field of activity is a standstill of flow.
Nature	When the sun sinks behind the mountain the earth sleeps.
Human	How does he steer his boat when there is no wind? He does not blow on the sail, he contemplates the stillness and how it strengthens him.
Form	When he raises laws between the good and the bad he imprisons rebirth.

13 Moving lines.

Fulfilment in difference.

Bottom line   On common ground difference is shared.
               Expression naturally flows from this
               in sharing separate experience.

Second line   He does not seek difference, but retires,
               seeking what is like. He gains no
               experience of what he is unlike.

Third line   Perhaps he thinks he is self reliant.
               He does not trust others to fill his
               lacking. This is a boundary of his
               awareness.

Fourth line   Beyond the boundary of his ego-self he
               accepts fulfilment in difference, widening
               his awareness.

Fifth line   It is hard to forgo priority for personal
               feelings, but accepting within them the
               different feelings of others creates an
               exciting and fulfilling flow between.

Top line   He finds a greater whole and he is
               inseparable. They are complementary.

Trigrams: Li, Sun, Ch'ien, Ch'ien.
The hesitant clings (Li) to the
firm (Sun) creating potential
(Ch'ien, Ch'ien). 13

Pattern   A transitory brightness
grows into the lasting,
indeed the eternal.

Nature   The fire is kindled
with the promise of wood.
The wood becomes radiant
only with fire.
Together they are like the sun.

Human   Living relationships
mean one fulfilling the other.
Recognition of complement
is attraction,
its activity, a stable pattern
of flow.

Form   Form is used,
transformed into brightness
in which the different
recognize each other
as part of one.
The wise ruler uses form thus.

14 Moving lines.

Fulfilment.

Bottom line	Activity is invited, but he is full of peace. In this mood he may find difficulty in forming new activity.
Second line	He can co-ordinate many things into action. This strength is the fulfilment of co-ordinating his own feelings.
Third line	Fulfilled, the ego-self requires nothing and so acts out for the benefit of the world. A needing self cannot get away from his need.
Fourth line	Aware of his wealth of fulfilment he is also aware of others' lack. He cannot help in this but there is no cause for guilt.
Fifth line	He knows himself just as himself. He does not consider the rich pattern of his many facets. How fortunate!
Top line	Reaching for a new canvas — he does not cease to expand experience.

Trigrams: Ch'ien, Ch'ien, Tui, Li. 14
Inner creative potential (Ch'ien,
Ch'ien) quickens (Tui) into a
personal brightness (Li at the top).

Pattern

Creative power
comes from the inner reaches
to shine on the returning tide
which possesses the day.

Nature

The sun shines all the day,
setting in glorious moments
for which it has prepared.

Human

The energy now comes
as the flow is inward.
It is a gift of beauty,
of power mellow from experience.

Form

The wise ruler becomes sage
whose certainty of touch
knows the outcome
after living the pattern.

15 ䷎ Moving lines.

Adapting to the flow.

Bottom line	The flow will carry him and he takes part, imposing nothing.
Second line	Satisfied for them to be what they will be, he is released from right and wrong. To maintain this broadens him.
Third line	He acts out the flow. Completing movements already there within him is harmonious.
Fourth line	Activity is not taken as his own. The movements are of the whole.
Fifth line	If he knows his strength he can still move positively, although among the many ways he moves he claims nothing.
Top line	Modesty as negation of what he is. He is not accepting the whole as himself. He is not understanding the flow as himself.

Trigrams: Kên, K'an, Chên, K'un.
The high (Kên) and the low
(K'an) fructify (Chên) the earth
(K'un).

Pattern   Rising up to the peak
and sinking to the abyss
is the cause of all activity.

Nature   The never ending motion of the sea
is its reality.

Human   By breathing in and out
he achieves life.
By moving between
exhaltation and despair
he achieves feeling.
By action and rest,
wellbeing.
By recognizing energy
and exhaustion
he completes things.

Form   Is transitory.

16 Moving lines.

In rest.

Bottom line	He has become deeply exhausted and has not the energy to prepare the next cycle.
Second line	So deep is his rest there is no activity among his possibilities. He cannot remain so for long.
Third line	He does not act out of his rest. Like a seed slow to germinate, he oversleeps.
Fourth line	Actively he accepts the world like a new morning. So much to be gained!
Fifth line	His feelings of the world are the link by which his body co-ordinates in his repose. Not accepting these feelings disorientates his functions. Taking himself to be in his world in new ways will alter this.
Top line	Resting even his needs, he will have no direction to flow. But they will be the first to waken.

Trigrams: K'un, Kên, K'an, Chên. The earth (K'un), the peak (Kên) and the abyss (K'an) are the power of (Chên) the return to potential (top trigram).

16

Pattern

The wave of life force
nourishes its source.

Nature

The seed
results from the growth
and decay of the plant.

Human

The sabbath,
the completion.
Each cycle has its period of rest.

Form

Without an amnesty
how is the knot to be untied?

17 Moving lines.

Becoming. New form.

Bottom line
He makes new forms on the open plain.
They are new realities to him;
Sharing them, they become more real.

Second line
No new form for his feelings.
He feels unchanged.
Unchanging lacks experience.

Third line
By acting out we change our skin,
but he holds back new growth,
not acting out the old.

Fourth line
Is he his skin?
Or is this only the boundary
of what he thinks he is.
To distinguish the superficial and the depth
is his guide.

Fifth line
Where are his feelings? Forming his form,
real to him. He can trust in this.

Top line
When not in transition he will teach.
Seeing his quietness they long to learn.

Trigrams: Chên, Kên, Sun, Tui.
To fructify (Chên) a high place
(Kên) gently and firmly (Sun),
awakens (Tui). 17

Pattern
    The high is fed from below.
This is service,
undemanding and constant,
becoming an awakening.

Nature
    Evolution is the devoted service
of life to a form.
It is form in service to life.

Human
    Our energy from inner depths
supports the highest place,
the widest view.
When established and firm
there are new realizations.

Form
    To serve, we follow.
We move towards that form,
becoming it.

18 Moving lines.

Decay.

Bottom line   To cease re-creating the old leads him
out if he has new to go to. His guide
would first start anew.

Second line   Feelings have become ingrown,
If he runs out too fast
he is likely to trip.

Third line   He makes his own road, finding established
ones overgrown. There is both resentment
and understanding.

Fourth line   In the long run it does not develop
him to continue in the way set out for
him. Old ways become exhausted.

Fifth line   Cannot live in the feeling of decay,
reacts by clearing up. Danger of
praise diverting.

Top line   When he sees decay for itself he no
longer works against it building always
grander forms. He loves it as he would
love the earth.

Trigrams: Sun, Tui, Chên, Kên.
Gentle inner life flow (Sun)
awakens (Tui) to a new active
spring (Chên) of high endeavour
(Kên).

Pattern

The source is firm,
formed and unflowing.
The outer form decays,
allowing a new to take its place.
Virile, rebuilding.

Nature

Maturity of autumn.
Sap thickens, dries.
Decay of winter.
Form dissipates.
Quickening of spring.
All is made new.

Human

Our ways are fixed
and move no more.
Allow their death
and walk away in new country.

Form

Perseverance in form,
momentum of habit,
pretence of life,
prevent reality living.

19 Moving lines.

Overgrowth.

Bottom line   He seeks to prepare shared integrated
                growth. This to avoid overgrowth.

Second line   Active in his feeling, where he is
                many-sided, he integrates there.
                This is to avoid overgrowth.

Third line   Not acting for fear of overgrowth.
                No path until he recognizes his fear.

Fourth line   He takes only a balance of things,
                not accepting the fast, sappy growth offered.

Fifth line   Seeing a field of immature growth he
                separates himself from it, knowing
                something better than this can give him.

Top line   There is no imbalance in his sharing.

Awakening (Tui) to spring (Chên)
throughout the earth (K'un) and
earthbound (K'un at the top).

19

Pattern   A time of happening approaches.
Lightness is in the air
flowing through every activity
as doors open
into space.

Nature   Intimations of spring
are everywhere.
Growth so rich
it will not flower.

Human   Flow into activity is unimpeded,
so free it knows no end.
So young it knows no maturing.

Form   Without regulation
form grows rampant.

20 Moving lines.

Wholeness.

Bottom line   Concentration on inner wholeness is right
for those who have not achieved it.
Only then is it possible, when inner
and outer are one, to have no inner
wholeness. Is he afraid to lose it?

Second line   Narrowing his view. He does not co-ordinate
his feelings; having only a slit view
at a time, he cannot feel them as a pattern.

Third line   He is not yet part of what is out there.
His view of himself determines this.
It cannot be otherwise.

Fourth line   Wholeness still means inside. He is not
yet ready to trust himself to the world.

Fifth line   Feeling his many selves, inner and outer,
as one, he meets his inner ego at the
borders of his consciousness and feels
more safe.

Top line   Accepting himself as the plain with no
conceptions his multitude of realities are
one. The life of the ego-self is the life of
the inner ego. He accepts his wholeness as
without limit.

Trigrams: K'un, K'un, Kên, Sun.
Inner activity (K'un) and outer
activity (K'un) and the
contemplation (Kên) of maturity
(Sun).

Pattern	The wide view from a height contemplates activity on and in the earth.
Nature	The mountain peak stands serene sloping down to valleys where life is teeming.
Human	Time of seeing the whole, of relating inner and outer life, quiet amongst activity but beyond it.
Form	See what is there. Take stock of it as a whole.

21   Moving lines.

Oppression.

Bottom line   The world has turned on him.
He seeks with those near him for harmony.

Second line   He has an inner advantage in being
oppressed, that is why he stays there.

Third line   His forces combat inside him, to his
discomfort. He has not the strength
to fight the outside.

Fourth line   Accepting oppression he has a lot to
put up with. Accepting that he has a
lot to put up with strengthens him.

Fifth line   He does not take his oppression to heart
but reacts with a wealth of secret activity.

Top line   Sharing out his oppression, he is hiding
in it. Hiding from freedom will make
him dull-witted.

21

Trigrams: Chên, Kên, K'an, Li.
Thunder within (Chên). High and
low oppose without (Kên, K'an).
Water and fire oppose on the
return (K'an, Li). The low is
opposed on all sides (Kên, K'an, Li).

Pattern	Grumbling discomfort
leads to oppression
of the lowly.
Nature	The earth quakes
beneath the mountain.
Rocks and fire
bombard the abyss.
Human	Inner discomfort erupts.
The weak have no escape
from the powerful,
who see in them the danger
of their own weakness.
Form	Law is formed to protect the weak,
used to satisfy the strong,
and controls the release of tension.
The wise judge knows
that wrong has no beginning,
and is fearless
in administering mercy.

Moving lines

Give way. Knowing both.

Bottom line   He does not hold his strength aloof,
but goes out to help preparations of others.
He does not want to be isolated.

Second line   He does not impose his feelings,
he may even hide them for hope of gain.

Third line   He gives away wholeheartedly, so that it
is noticed.

Fourth line   His motive is not coloured by desires.
Though he would like to give way he cannot
because of a principle he has learned.

Fifth line   Among his feelings he has not enough
strength or breadth of vision to be
graceful while giving way.

Top line   While giving passage as a natural right
he takes himself as he may be, which is
the grace of truth.

Trigrams: Li, K'an, Chên, Kên.
The opposition of fire (Li) and
water (K'an) has release (Chên),
giving a wide view (Kên).

Pattern   When a wider view prevails,
             releasing tension between opposites,
             there is a giving way gracefully.

Nature   The sea moves
             under the moon
             under the sun
             and gains its strength.

Human   To give way,
             to allow passage,
             is to know your strength,
             not squandering it
             in small matters.

Form   Projection of a living self
             into form
             confuses the flowing field
             with the poles.

23 Moving lines.

Solitude.

Bottom line | Inaction causes a solitude that faces nothing.
Continued inaction makes him nothing.
Any movement is better than no movement.

Second line | How can he reach others without co-ordination
of feeling? He faces no pattern, continuing
without pattern disintegrates.
Doing simple things together is the basis
of arrangement.

Third line | When he was with them he was alone.
He does not go out to them. This makes
way for a solution.

Fourth line | Not accepting them as part of him he cannot
recognize himself, not knowing himself he
feels alone.
He rejects in them what he rejects in himself.
In need of an amnesty to unlock the danger.

Fifth line | He does not accept the feeling of solitude.
Finding a group like himself he no longer
feels alone.

Top line | In order to manage being alone he does not
feel lonely, although not nourished by a
feeling of wholeness.
Inside (behind consciousness) he shares and
is carried. Outside he builds protection
and is separated.

Trigrams: K'un, K'un, K'un, Kên. Inner activity (K'un) and outer activity (K'un, K'un) gives a return (top trigram) to solitude (Kên).

Pattern	When inner activity pervades all outer activity we find ourselves in solitude.
Nature	To spin a cocoon heralds inner change and chrysalis.
Human	Each into himself. Each unto himself leaves nothing to share.
Form	When there are no bonds things do not remain together.

24 Moving lines.

Return and make new.

Bottom line   Preparing renewal even before the old is
acted out he ensures a continuous flow of
activity. He need not worry that he has
this sensitivity, although it may induce worry.

Second line   Allowing existing ways to peter out before
starting anew. Peaceful transitions
without tension.

Third line   Doing things differently yet they are the
same. Not acting out he returns to his ego-
self, to go out again unchanged. This
self is the actor not the author.

Fourth line   Without feedback there cannot be co-ordination.
If there is no feedback they are the wrong
people.

Fifth line   He has the courage to remove his feelings
from it and walk away. There is relief and
new beginnings.

Top line   He has nothing to guide him. Not learning
the essence of his experience his actions
become hazardous.

Trigrams: Chên, K'un, K'un, K'un.
Arousal (Chên) of activity (K'un)
in the earth (K'un) returning (top
trigram) to the earth (K'un). 24

Pattern
That which arises
returns to its source.

Nature
The nature of nature
in the earth.

Human
To the place where we have been
we return.
To the mood we lived
we return.
Returning is arising anew.

Form
Returning to a form
we re-form it
and make it new.
By this
the form of society evolves.

25 Moving lines.

Natural innocence.

Bottom line   Not possessing, he shares without effort,
without any drive in his need. Harmonious.

Second line   His awareness is widened if he does not
co-ordinate towards goals. He will not
stagnate if he ceases to invest his present
in the future.

Third line   Seeing no need, his ego-self is inactive.
All realities are activities in their own
terms, so he loses strength in his outer
reality; others take the initiative from him.

Fourth line   Accepting ego action without an ego-self
need he can accomplish things without
narrowing his reality.

Fifth line   Accepting feeling without need is to achieve
natural innocence. Feeling without feeling
need involves reorganizing the way he
nourishes himself. Disorientation, then
reorientation.

Top line   If he accepts this inner reality without
involvement where is he involved? Here
his involvement originates, whatever its form.

The thunderstorm (Chên) comes
to the mountain (Kên) which,
firm and gentle (Sun), remains
tranquil (Ch'ien).

25

Pattern

Confusion does not disturb
those without involvement.

Nature

When the storm roars
the animal sleeps
in its dry cave.

Human

Purified of motive
has no need
with which to fear.

Innocence
holds the hand of anger smiling,
steps lightly through confusion.

Form

The need of form
makes ways to map.
Mapped confusion — guile.

26 Moving lines.

The flow and the channel.

Bottom line There is a natural strong flow into action.
It does not need preparing. Danger of the
channel thinking it ought to be the flow, this
forms ego-centric actions.

Second line There is a natural strong flow into action.
He is held back by co-ordinating his feelings
about it when his progress depends upon letting
it flow through him.

Third line The flow is in action. He watches the flow.
He helps the flow, not identifying himself
with it. If he is vigilant in this it is
most rewarding.

Fourth line He does not confuse his ego-self with the
source; not accepting the flow as his own
he is free of entangling aggression.

Fifth line He is open to awareness of new feelings
because he does not feel himself as creator.

Top line Recognizing this inner plain as the source
of the flow. Recognizing the outer activity
as the channel. Recognizing that he is both
his reality becomes open ended.

26

Trigrams: Ch'ien, Tui, Chên, Kên.
Inner life force (Ch'ien) has an
idea (Tui), breaks into activity
(Chên) and makes a mountain
(Kên).

Pattern	Great actions achieve their purpose. Outer obeys inner, becoming quiet and still.
Nature	Life force unfolds in evolution of form. The peak of form is order.
Human	He is inspired. Works all day outside, discovering the form of things he thinks he has made. In the evening he sits on the mountain.
Form	The pipe through which water flows.

27 Moving lines.

Choice from the flow.

Bottom line — Returns after achieving open view
preparing activity to hide in.
When hidden feels imprisoned.
No cause for guilt in freedom.

Second line — Here feelings co-ordinate to make direction.
He does not use this channel, seeking
to know without feeling experience —
yet he came to feel.

Third line — If his ego-self is not active he does not
expand his experience, he is not nourished.
His ego-self can be active without being
possessive.

Fourth line — Not accepting the ego-self path as his
total reality, he opens his view to all
his possibilities and has an appetite for
taking in new ways of being.

Fifth line — Why does he refuse the reality his feelings
show him? Continuing to feel, he needs to
answer that.

Top line — He brought with him certain challenges. Finding
he has reality other than these in the quietness
of his being should not distract him from
meeting them with effort.

Trigrams: Chên, K'un, K'un, Kên.
From the inner life force activity
flows (Chên) throughout the
earth (K'un, K'un) leaving passive
form (Kên).

Pattern   All action has results in form.
           All growth towards the archetypes.

Nature   Storm and torrents flow.
           In every crevice watered
           something grows.
           Every crack eroded shows
           what has passed:
           each hollow filled,
           another shape.

Human   From what passes through
           we are made.
           From what we choose
           we are nourished
           according to our need.

Form   To provide what others need
           to fill their form,
           follow the pattern of their choice.
           For our own we follow ours.

28 Moving lines.

Rigidity.

Bottom line | Where it has become very firm, prepare to be unbiased and gently supporting. This will produce harmony.

Second line | Opening to feeling, the sap flows once again — feeling relief and wellbeing.

Third line | That which is rigid tends to be brittle.
Acting out amongst rigidity disrupts.
Disruption is unfortunate.
The unfortunate is sometimes necessary.

Fourth line | Recognizing rigidity in his outer environment, he makes allowances and does not cause the situation to break apart.

Fifth line | Recognizing feeling as having become rigid allows it to flower again. This flowering is replacing past mischance and does not carry present life flow into fruit. It is, however, making up for something lost.

Top line | He does not realize the depth of his reality, that is why it overwhelms him.
However deep his recognition this sometimes happens, as his reality has no imposed boundaries.

Trigrams: Sun, Ch'ien, Ch'ien, Tui.
Becoming firm (Sun), the creative
(Ch'ien) is stilled (Ch'ien), giving
joy of a beginning (Tui).

Pattern	From the inner there is no flow. Action is all inactivity, making return a beginning.
Nature	The wood is too ripe for budding, too rigid for change until it returns to earth.
Human	When firm, inflexible, the only way of moving is to break. When so gentle it changes nothing, the only way of living is to die into a beginning.
Form	No longer supported must fall. Falling, finds support.

29 Moving lines.

The unfamiliar.

Bottom line	Increasing focus in alien conditions because he does not prepare his feelings to flow.
Second line	When co-ordinating many unfamiliar feelings he must move with care because he lacks points of reference.
Third line	He has no place to stand in the unfamiliar yet he needs to see his way before acting. First he must take stock of his position.
Fourth line	The way to avoid being lost in the unfamiliar is to look at its components. It is then realized that these are familiar and their arrangement is alien. Then his awareness is nourished by them.
Fifth line	Recognizing familiar feelings which make up his alien situation he no longer feels overwhelmed, he can cope with it.
Top line	He only sees what is familiar in an alien situation. This confines his awareness until he changes.

Water (K'an) flows out (Chên), is
made still, held up (Kên) and
reappears (K'an).

29

Pattern   Downward flow resisted.
Fitful progress
must be passed through.

Nature   Water flows into low places
and overflows
around rocks
and on.

Human   Away from the familiar.
Pitfalls and barriers
endanger the weary.
Continue flowing out
and overflow them,
passing danger by.

Form   Not recognizing a downward path
he promises a high place
and is confused.

30 Moving lines.

Clinging to the real.

Bottom line
Which, for him, is the real, the need that prepares for activity or the activity which results from the need? Yet whichever it is, he progresses.

Second line
His feelings give him insight into his activities. He does not co-ordinate them for purposes, he uses them as judge. As they stand central in the spectrum of his reality this gives him balance.

Third line
Clinging to the reality of his ego-self he either abandons himself to it or curses its limited time. Either way he is limited.

Fourth line
When he accepts the ego-self as reality it seems that he appears from nowhere and has no purpose. Actions that arise only in this ego-self do not carry his life flow and seem like this also.

Fifth line
He does not go far from the real. When he does not accept the reality of his feelings they become pent up and then pour through him, claiming their reality.

Top line
Clinging to his inner ego as his real source leads him to feel his ego-self as false. The ego is found to be real but misled into considering itself.

Trigrams: Li, Sun, Tui, Li.
Hesitant flame (Li) becomes
constant with wood (Sun) giving
birth (Tui) to new fire (Li).

30

Pattern

Brightness is part of transition
of the firm and ripened
into the new,
which has a new brightness.

Brightness depends upon fuel,
transition upon brightness,
bright new form upon transition.

Nature

From a spark the forest flames.
From the ashes all grows new.

Human

Clinging to the real,
fitfully,
he shines through shadows
of his form.
Consuming his reality
reveals an essence
brighter than his spark of faith.

Form

Form transmutes,
welcomes death.

31 Moving lines.

Coming out of himself.

Bottom line	The idea is very far from his mind. He is shy of even preparing it, but it is there.
Second line	Acting now may reinforce his shyness: because his feelings are not yet co-ordinated about it he may become confused.
Third line	He should be wary of the weak: when he first acts out of his shyness he looks for support and they will answer. Acting out of shyness requires its own strength.
Fourth line	He accepts his outward movement firmly as himself. Ceasing to hover on the threshold strengthens his relationship with others.
Fifth line	Accepting reality in the outflow of his feelings he is released from tension.
Top line	Over-compensating shyness. He does not face it fully.

Trigrams: Kên, Sun, Ch'ien, Tui.
Still in the beginning, dormant
(Kên) ripens (Sun) into the
creative (Ch'ien) joy (Tui).

31

Pattern   When the shy gains strength
to meet the unfamiliar
needs are satisfied.

Nature   When the lake is full
it flows out,
watering the land.

Human   Time to take the hand
that is there.
Time to fulfil lacking.

Form   Creating with joy is
finding that things fit together.
Mating.

32 Moving lines.

Continuing. Branching out.

Bottom line   Insufficient preparation, branching out
before he is ready he has not enough weight
to carry it through.

Second line   He gains relief, flowing through his feelings.
The burden of rigidity is cast off.

Third line   Losing himself in the world, he branches out
by proliferating outer activities. By doing
this he will see less and less.

Fourth line   He makes his reality in the outer world.
Continuing in the transitory is not nourishing.

Fifth line   Accepting that he does not branch out in
his feelings, keeping to one channel.
Thus he develops constancy rather than
adventurousness.

Top line   Not branching out, he will have to continue
by repeating activity. This carries no
life force.

Trigrams: Sun, Ch'ien, Tui, Chên.
The mature (Sun) creates (Ch'ien)
joy (Tui) by returning with new
life (Chên at the top).

Pattern
A new cycle
comes from the old.
It does not wither
but continues,
producing new growth.

Nature
From mature wood
new strong shoots
continue to appear.

Human
More than one life in life.
Maturity does not stagnate,
middle age no signal of decline.
Youth continues in the old.

Form
By continual renewal
living form has duration.
By exceptional renewal,
Rejuvenation.

Moving lines.

Withdrawal.

Bottom line   He does not prepare his withdrawal, which
leaves him in an exposed position. He is
too taken with the idea of advance.

Second line   He is so bound up in the idea of advance
he has no feeling for retreat. Only seeing
in one direction narrows him.

Third line   He attracts attention to his withdrawal,
needing activity. This can successfully
protect his feelings of inferiority.

Fourth line   He who has inner awareness sometimes withdraws
from outer activity, but for he who is real
only in outer activity withdrawal is defeat.

Fifth line   Accepting the feeling of withdrawal he
retreats willingly. This is a change of
direction.

Top line   He who can see the complete horizon retreats
happily in any direction.

Stillness within (Kên), firmness
and tranquillity in the active (Sun,
Ch'ien), and tranquil returning
(Ch'ien).

Pattern

There is no movement outward.
Restraint where action might be
and a quiet withdrawal.
Outside forces are not opposed.

Nature

Deer graze in a clearing.
Prowling cats.
There are more shadows
in the forest.

Human

There is no judgement on retreat.
It is the natural flow.
To oppose now
is opposing our own pattern.
To fight is weaponless.
In withdrawing
the return is creative.

Form

When we have not the means
we cannot seek ends.
Rather use what is at hand.

34 Moving lines.

A store of power.

Bottom line To use his power always preparing for the future weakens his ever-present present.

Second line To accomplish many things at once requires great co-ordination of feeling, and teaches immeasurably.

Third line He charges down a road single-minded, getting so involved with it he is not free to make decisions.

Fourth line He distinguishes between himself and his power for outer action and becomes free to choose its use. All controlled activity revolves around this discovery, all progress involves its use. Through it he ceases to identify himself in his outside activity.

Fifth line A feeling of power. He does not accept its use. He is released from a troublesome beast. He touches the root of wisdom.

Top line Not recognizing the source of his power he has no power to act. I speak to him but he is talking and does not hear me. He has only to turn his head.

Inner tranquillity (Ch'ien)
continued into the active (Ch'ien)
makes the buds (Tui) of new
growth (Chên).

Pattern   He watches.
Comes late into action
with the power
of great potential.

Nature   The seed
with great stores
awaits in tranquillity,
then bursts upon the world.

Human   Slowly absorbing experience.
Quietly relating inner and outer.
Great power for action
when we are ready.

Form   Powerful government knows
the flexibility of new ideas
woven between the mature.

35 Moving lines.

Primal forces create change.

Bottom line   Change overtakes him, appearing as a setback
              in his way, but the change is basic, he was
              not prepared for it.

Second line   Change wells up in his feelings. He is not
              in control here and it causes him distress.
              If he co-ordinates his feelings instead of
              controlling them this same change would
              cause him happiness.

Third line   When his basic way of being is changing
              it is harmonious for him to act within,
              not to make changes outside.

Fourth line   When his inner reality is changing it is
              inappropriate to put his faith in outer
              activity that he created before. An awkward
              moment in transition. It is harmonious to
              be widely aware and not carry over.

Fifth line   When primal change is happening it is
              harmonious to suspend acceptance of feedback
              from the old.

Top line   Accepting change at the foundation involves
              changing the superstructure. This is demanding
              and needs the approach of sympathy.

35

Trigrams: K'un, Kên, K'an, Li.
Activity in the earth (K'un) raises
a mountain (Kên), forms an abyss
(K'an) with fire (Li).

Pattern

Formation.
Primal forces
in the making of things.

Nature

The earth heaves
restlessly,
reshaped by its own power
of the depths.

Human

He makes himself anew,
his karma moving
into new relationship
accomplishes his growth.

Form

Control of change
occurring of itself
is the hinge of power.

36 Moving lines.

Effort through resistance.

Bottom line   The world does not nourish him, but he
               continues to flow outwards. Have a care,
               without caring.

Second line   He finds uses for his feelings as they appear.
               He rides life, reacting to its movements, which
               he cannot co-ordinate at this time. Learning
               to ride life gives freedom.

Third line   Acting out to overcome resistance he finds
               eventually that his efforts were being absorbed
               by resistance of his own. He controls the
               outside but it takes some time to find that
               this is a reflection of what is inside.

Fourth line   When his outgoing efforts are continually
               absorbed, his inner realities are dominant
               and he turns his attention to these.

Fifth line   Although his effects are absorbed his cause
               is not. His feelings remain real to him
               because they are not absorbed — they are
               not absorbed because he does not show them.

Top line   Turning away from a challenge he had set
               himself. He has allowed them to exhaust him
               and seeks rest. He can take rest without
               abandoning his path.

Trigrams: Li, K'an, Chên, K'un.
Inner fire (Li) moves the water
(K'an), making new activity
(Chên) returning earth (K'un).

Pattern
Outward movement
of the life force
is opposed but not quenched.
Its work in the opposition itself
is creating life
to the benefit of the world.

Nature
Earth-fire under water
does not shine.
The seas boil.
New islands appear.

Human
He cannot achieve his purpose,
turns his frustration
to lasting benefit for others.

Form
Efforts are absorbed
by fluidity of form.
Continuing the effort
enables unexpected forms
to appear.

37 Moving lines.

Nourishing relationships.

Bottom line   Activity towards complementary relationships gives no insecurity. There is harmony and helping.

Second line   Little things are important when feeling does not flow and relationships appear not to nourish. Attend to these little things.

Third line   When he acts out for himself in relationship the relationship must allow for this. He must allow for the relationship. Otherwise there is loss of sympathy.

Fourth line   When he does not see relationship by his own light it has a harmonious balance.

Fifth line   Interweaving his feelings amongst them he does not choose any favourite. There is no cause for insecurity.

Top line   Making his reality amongst nourishing relationships gives a flexible strength which is more acceptable to others when it has mellowed.

Trigrams: Li, K'an, Li, Sun.
Fire (Li) passes through water
(K'an, Li) gentle and matured
(Sun).

Pattern   Opposites alternate in harmony,
gently maturing.

Nature   Sun and rain.
Nature grows and ripens.

Human   The taming of fire
made home.
The fire of opposites dancing together
becomes life rhythm.
The young and hesitant
grow mature.
The fluid pattern of family life
grows firm, even rigid.

Form   The ordering of things
so each plays its part
establishes order in the whole.

38 Moving lines.

Opposition in time. (Taking turns.)

Bottom line He moves into limiting opposites purposely to experience. This temporary loss of freedom has purpose and is an intentional ignorance.

Second line He must give way but cannot see a way through. His way cannot have precedence. Opposites need to be accepted.

Third line There is opposition and he is not active, which is humiliating. He is not using his individual freedom to oppose. Later he finds a way and feels relief.

Fourth line Accepting opposition as being reality is accepting isolation from other people, but this also accepts their separate value. This is being a form, which he came to do, does not like, and changes.

Fifth line Understanding the root of the matter, he does not have his reality in opposites. Treating opposite tendencies as having a single cause he does not choose between them. Having this wide view enables him to accomplish.

Top line Seeing a reality that encompasses opposites makes warring opposition seem wrong. But it is wiser to allow people to find out than to teach them.

Trigrams: Tui, Li, K'an, Li.
Awakening (Tui) to fire (Li) and
water (K'an) and fire (Li).

38

Joy (Tui) flames up (Li), is
quenched (K'an), and flames
again (Li).

Pattern

Forces of opposition
cannot coexist
without losing character,
so they take turns.

Nature

The cosmos
moves in cycles
of the active and the tranquil.

Human

To move with the easy
and rest simply
in harmony with others
allows his actions to be his own.

When the young
realize taking turns
they can express fully
without frustration.

Form

To realize form
is to allow its innate character.
Wise government
is not imposed.

39   Moving lines.

Upheaval.

Bottom line | He needs to wait for less extreme conditions so he does not prepare for activity yet.

Second line | His feelings are extreme and variable and he does not attempt co-ordination but works through as best he can. His feelings are only reacting to conditions.

Third line | He tries to impose his way on the chaos, but with his environment in upheaval he cannot keep a direction.

Fourth line | He does not associate himself with the upheaval of his environment and remains undisturbed. Because he is steady amongst instability people come to him.

Fifth line | In his feelings he goes with the extreme movements. At extremes there is a comradeship born of isolation from the mass.

Top line | He needs to interpret each situation as it arrives according to his own light. He is capable of this because he has not involved himself deeply in the prevailing chaos.

Trigrams: Ken, K'an, Li, K'an.
Emerging life force remains still
(Ken) in the face of warring
opposites (K'an, Li, K'an).

39

The high is set against the low (Ken,
K'an). Water quenches fire (K'an,
Li). The bright is in the abyss (Li,
K'an).

Pattern

The life force halts
when each tries to take
the other's place.

Nature

In upheaval.
The water is upon the land.
The mountain in the water.
Fire springs from chasms.
The life force waits its time.

Human

They fight around him.
He does not take part,
knowing other ways.

Form

When the outside forces
are attacking one another
form is overthrown.

40 Moving lines.

Release from indecision.

Bottom line	He leaves his way open to circumstance. Riding life, he has freedom.
Second line	An active direction removes suspicions that eroded his positive feelings. He can move now and will need some discretion to be successful.
Third line	Acting out of the ego-self possesses, first an I, then adds to it in excess. His only release from this is when it is taken from him.
Fourth line	He makes his own path his reality, neglecting the other. He accepts both and meets himself in the other.
Fifth line	Offered release he dare not move. He has become accustomed to his walls and closes his feelings. He can, however, have confidence in release.
Top line	He looks neither on stress nor on release (in the mind one preys upon the other) and is released from the cycle of alternate stress and release.

Trigrams: K'an, Li, K'an, Chên. 40
A swing of opposites (K'an, Li,
K'an) breaks into free movement
(Chên).

Pattern   A new way leads out of
                 insecurity and vacillation.
                 Release from indecision.

Nature   Torrential rain — mud.
                 Baking sun — rock.
                 Torrents again — mud.
                 Stress
                 between earth and heaven
                 flashes lightning
                 and is no more.
                 Delicate tendrils, messengers,
                 can feel their way again.

Human   Taking both.
                 Allowing tension through him,
                 not dodging it,
                 he comes to decision
                 and is released.

Form   Uncertainty of direction
                 is oscillation faster
                 than complete action.
                 Taking in both
                 damps vibrations.

41 Moving lines.

Failure of expectation.

Bottom line   He is planning new activity to replace
the old. There are other people here
to be considered.

Second line   Seeking satisfaction for need — seeking
a gain. It fails to satisfy inner needs
for a change in feeling experience.
Seeking action in which he sees no gain for
himself releases him into this change.

Third line   Uncertain, he is not active. Everything
becomes a choice. If he sought complements
he could take both.

Fourth line   Re-examining his expectations relaxes his
focus on them and releases a flow from
his inner self.

Fifth line   He learns the supreme lesson of failure,
unimportant in itself and important in the
changes it produces. He takes what he can just
sense as more real than what he fully feels.
This can hatch a harmonious change of his
feeling.

Top line   Accepting the inner meaning of failure of
expectation; that reality is dynamic, expectation
fixed — a narrow extract from reality.

41

Trigrams: Tui, Chên, K'un, Kên.
Birth (Tui) of a new form (Chên)
in the earth (K'un) returns as
stillness (Kên).

Pattern	Starts with great promise, grows with vigour, has no offspring.
Nature	The crop fails.
Human	No outcome. After growth, no activity of fertility. No coming together of diversity. Where has he gone? Into the stillness. How did he reach it? Giving up both.
Form	Not to expect the unexpected is the natural failure of those who plan.

42 Moving lines.

Strength to accomplish challenges.

Bottom line   He sets himself difficult tasks and has the
strength to fulfil them. Fortunate and
harmonious.

Second line   His strength is in the natural pattern of
his feelings, he does not need to co-ordinate
them. It is said he has a gift.

Third line   He does not take on an external challenge.
This is not through weakness, despite
appearances. His challenge is to be able
to refrain.

Fourth line   Without accepting external challenges he
turns his strength to feel and examine his
inner reality. He can find the last links
of thought that complete a chain, which
releases him.

Fifth line   It is more harmonious for him to accept the
challenges of emotional levels than seeing how
his many experiences fit together.

Top line   Allowing his strength to be used by one of his
weaknesses, he accepts challenges as a way of
being. Getting lost in challenging everything
will set people against him.

42

Trigrams: Chên, K'un, Kên, Sun.
Inner life force activates (Chên)
the earth (K'un) becoming
tranquil (Kên) and mature (Sun).

Pattern
The flow of life seeks the high,
becoming firm yet gentle,
resisting indulgence.
In seeking the highest
the low is fulfilled.

Nature
On the mountain
the tree grows strong sinews
while nourishing the slopes.

Human
Knowing he has power,
he accomplishes great tasks.
Not for himself
but he is strengthened.

Form
Seeking the easy
weakens into difficulty.
Working in the difficult
grows an easy strength.

43 Moving lines.

A peak of accumulation.

Bottom line
When there is great potential stored up it is
not the time for preparation, but for action.
That he still prepares indicates that he plans
something greater than he has strength for.

Second line
He has the power to flow out; why does he search
his feelings for signs and ways? They have
become obscured in disuse. Fear not, a river
makes its own course.

Third line
How can he help getting caught in his own flow
as it breaks out? It is natural in this
situation to be too forcefully himself.

Fourth line
Needing to flow out he cannot accept moderation
nor the lead of others. He arouses enmity by
accepting his forceful path as his way and this
makes it hard for him.

Fifth line
He accepts his flowing along emotional paths.
If he discriminates between the harmonious and
the discordant this releases him.

Top line
It will come upon him suddenly. He is not
recognizing the need for release. Blind
forces cause destruction when unseen.

Trigrams: Ch'ien, Ch'ien, Ch'ien, Tui.
The creative potential (Ch'ien) is not transformed into activity (Ch'ien, Ch'ien) but returns (top trigram) joyfully, knowing activity is at hand (Tui).

Pattern   The power of the creative
           withholds action,
           building up such a store
           it brims over.

Nature   The lake has risen,
           it must flow out
           and water the land.

Human   A time of accumulation reaches its peak.
           The time for giving out has come.
           There is power enough.

Form   When the rich and powerful
           do not support
           the poor and weak,
           catastrophe threatens.

44 Moving lines.

Adapting to circumstances.

Bottom line   He is held back in preparation. Feeling he cannot
              get on, yet he should not try. He must himself
              change.

Second line   Emotionally adapting to circumstances, he feels
              contained (literally he has to contain himself)
              but this is in harmony with his progress.

Third line   He learns to respect circumstances by experience.
              Not bowing to circumstance makes his way like
              walking waist high in thorn scrub.

Fourth line   There is no living quality in him if he adopts
              adaptation as outer action. Outer change alone
              leads to splitting.

Fifth line   He accepts ever changing patterns of feeling
              as he adapts to situations. At first he is
              not nourished, then he finds he is riding life.

Top line   Headlong adaptation, like a sudden giving way,
              appears as weakness but often comes from strength

Trigrams: Sun, Ch'ien, Ch'ien, Ch'ien.

44

Inner maturity (Sun, bottom trigram) remains tranquil in activity (Ch'ien, Ch'ien) and returns equally tranquil (Ch'ien at the top).

Pattern   The powerfully mature
comes to activity.
Without being influenced
has influence.

Nature   The flow of oceans
does not yield to our swimming.
The place of planets
does not shift for our desire.

Human   He does not try to change
what is so formed,
but meeting it
he is so drawn
he must himself change.

Form   All forms have archetypes
they tend towards,
yet the archetype
has no form.

45 Moving lines.

Out of gestation.

Bottom line   He needs faith in a coming birth. He need not fear, has no reason to falter, preparation has already been made.

Second line   Feelings grow in secret. Be aware of them, give them room for expression.

Third line   He cannot, by outside action, bring on a new birth, but he need not sit and do nothing. A rhythm of activity was made for this need.

Fourth line   His outer self is also the new life within. Identifying with it makes the flow easy and harmonious.

Fifth line   With experience he can feel what he needs to feed his growth. It is by sensing these needs and becoming aware of his feelings that trust in them becomes established.

Top line   Growth is going on within him but he cannot accept it and feels needlessly sad.

Trigrams: K'un, Kên, Sun, Tui.
Emerging activity (K'un at the
bottom) in stillness (Kên)
maturing (Sun), pregnant (Tui). 45

Pattern   Gestation.
           New life being formed in seclusion.
           Gathering together,
           preparing for a birth.

Nature   In an egg, when a bird.
           In a womb, when a mammal.
           In the sky, when a storm gathering.

Human   Idea gathers in mind's womb
           impregnated with experience.
           Human form in the female
           aroused by the male.
           In secret its soul enters,
           the essence of its total.

Form   Forming form
           is delicate,
           takes its own time hidden.
           To intrude endangers it.

46 Moving lines.

New growth out of maturity.

Bottom line   To make new branches he does not need new roots.
               He can do this from his accumulated being with
               ease and harmony.

Second line   When his reality is truly in his feelings this
               activity will bring him joy. If he is tempted
               to babble it brings him discredit.

Third line   He takes possession of his world as the leaves
               of a tree are its summer form. If he seeks
               no gain he remains free.

Fourth line   He seeks no return from his personal path, no
               gain to himself. Why? His ego-self has seen itself
               and is happily beyond its will to grow.

Fifth line   His feeling for growing out falters — never
               mind, it is still there.

Top line   Talk not of ends, there is only change.
               He is reality and need not narrow it in
               order to rest. If he had not thought of
               ends he would have rested sooner.

Trigrams: Sun, Tui, Chên, K'un. The mature (Sun) buds (Tui) into new growth (Chên), making activity late in the cycle (K'un at the top).

Pattern	After accumulating there is much power for activity later.
Nature	When roots are strong in the earth they push up great growth. New shoots from old stock.
Human	He has gathered and assimilated experience. He can now turn this into many forms. He is mature yet young.
Form	Wealth has been made. How to use it wisely? Nature makes growth in new directions.

47 Moving lines.

Exhaustion of activity.

Bottom line   He has lived through it. His interest is exhausted.
               If he thinks he is his interest he himself feels
               exhausted and prepares no change. Only change
               will free his flow.

Second line   Autumn is not followed by spring. Because he has
               gathered his crop he feels an end, wishing at
               once to sow another. He must feed his land and
               maintain things, then he will be ready.

Third line   He loses interest and ceases to act. He has
               exhausted his ego activity yet still seeks a basis
               for his reality there. Everything will appear to
               oppose him. In this way his inner ego forces him
               to seek more widely.

Fourth line   He used his wealth as the vehicle of his life
               and reached the end of doing that. This end
               is a beginning that will come from inside.

Fifth line   Accepting exhaustion in his feelings, he is unable
               to move. By fixing on what is exhausted he loses
               guidance and dignity. Seeing this, he can reach
               for his inner knowing that his ways are
               inexhaustible.

Top line   Not accepting that activity is exhausted, he presses
               on in an inefficient way, resenting it. Time
               to stop — and start.

Trigrams: K'an, Li, Sun, Tui.
Primal water (K'an at the
bottom) and fire (Li) matures
(Sun) into an awakening (Tui).

47

Pattern

Basic forces of opposition
change into the firm
through exhaustion
of their activity.

Nature

When the seas boil
in fissures of fire
this is too extreme
for the delicate tissues of life;
but when this force is spent,
life begins.

Human

He misunderstands exhaustion,
building walls is exhausted
not the builder.
Constructing the roof
uses other means not yet tapped.

When building walls is exhausted
they are high enough.
If he continues higher
he is pretending.

Form

The completion of a form
is always the condition
for the start of another.
Exhaustion is its signal.

48 Moving lines.

Bringing out the life within.

Bottom line · A phase of his living is at an end, yet he is
not preparing a new flow. He need not confuse
himself with his activity.

Second line · He uses actions to take the place of emotional
flow, but as he moves through these his more
natural flow will reappear.

Third line · He acts out of his ego-self, which benefits
not even himself. A miser is not made great
by his wealth. To own the life force is to
stop its flow.

Fourth line · He clears the channels through which he flows
by ending his belief that the life force
flowing through him is his own.

Fifth line · Opening his feelings to what life offers him
his flow is free and uninhibited.

Top line · He sees that his source is within, that his life
does not come to him from outside. He now has
the means of reaching his life energy and can
achieve without becoming exhausted.

Trigrams: Sun, Tui, Li, K'an.
Gently, constantly (Sun) it is
ready to flow out (Tui), holding
back yet giving (Li) water (K'an).

48

Pattern

At the source it is constant,
ready to give forth;
but it clings to its source.
Too gentle to overcome opposition
without help it cannot flow.

Nature

Not all the animals at the waterhole
have means to reach the water,
but nature grows ways
to achieve necessities.

Human

He is shy
yet has much to give.
When persuaded to flow
he nourishes all around him.

Form

Obtaining water from a well
takes some effort
some equipment
some skill.

49 Moving lines.

Breaking out of the old.

Bottom line	Inner activity is preparing for a new start. It is well hidden.
Second line	He does not co-ordinate his feelings in his usual manner, to do so would bring out the old pattern. When he has completed the change, it will be obvious and clear.
Third line	Acting out, it is difficult for him to distinguish the old from the new. He has new within but he needs more change before he can bring it out. He must not hurry this.
Fourth line	A change becomes real to him and he needs to change the way he does things to be in sympathy with this.
Fifth line	He knows change by nuance in his feelings. If he were to accomplish this completely he would be, himself, his oracle. Be gentle with power.
Top line	He does not accept a change of form. It is his choice. When living the essence and acting the form, change is a new dress for the actor. When living the form unconscious of the essence, he appears himself to change. Acting while not accepting change is unfruitful. Action creates change.

Trigrams: Li, Sun, Ch'ien, Tui.
Fire (Li) coming upon wood
(Sun) is that which creates
(Ch'ien) the emerging (Tui).

49

Pattern

The bright,
belonging in the new,
needs something mature to change
before reaching fulfilment.

Nature

The snake
renews its skin
when the old
is no longer flexible enough
for him to grow.

Human

When he has invested himself
in his life
he must divest himself
to start anew.

Form

When the old form
will not change enough
the lower revolts and destroys
to form the new.

50 Moving lines.

Integration.

Bottom line To allow one thing to finish entirely before starting another allows a clean start. If there is difficulty in starting again, accept the disadvantages and get on with it.

Second line He relates causes and effects within his feelings, giving him an inner nourishment not understood by those around him. His awareness widens though no new fact is added.

Third line Changing the outer appearance does not nourish him. Relief will come when he feels reality in what he does. This is the flow from inside.

Fourth line By accepting outer reality as the one where his happiness lies he co-ordinates that for satisfaction. He does not see that the inner entirely supports the outer, and loses that support. Pay attention to what is hidden, not what is obvious.

Fifth line Neglecting the impact of feeling as a way of knowing, he grasps with understanding at the practical definitions of knowledge. He sharpens his awareness but has need to widen it.

Top line By using the co-ordination of his levels as his way of being he has a hold on understanding that gives gentle endurance to his activities. Because of this they flourish.

Trigrams: Sun, Ch'ien, Tui, Li.
Gentle, maturing (Sun), tranquil
creativity (Ch'ien) is pregnant
with (Tui) bright flame (Li).

50

Pattern   Steady unwavering preparation
            makes enlightenment possible.

Nature   The bird carefully chooses
            when building its nest
            in which to nurture its young.

Human   He persists constantly
            in melding together
            his life's ingredients.
            This alchemy
            transforms his awareness.

Form   Continuous interaction
            of individuals in society
            nourishes an awareness
            of the whole.

51 Moving lines.

Shaken in his being.

Bottom line	It comes too fast for recognition. Suddenly! Oh what shall we do? — As suddenly it is our friend.
Second line	So shaken he cannot co-ordinate his feelings. He is scattered and vulnerable. The nature of shock is short-lived, when it is over he becomes himself again.
Third line	So shaken he cannot act. Shock causes his withdrawal. His stress is relieved if he can recognize shock and act through it.
Fourth line	Accepting shock as a way of action makes confusion. The nature of shock is spontaneous, using it to manipulate his environment will turn that environment against him.
Fifth line	Not allowing himself to feel shock, he feels threatened, but the danger in shock is transitory and over before he starts to worry. If he is active he will see this.
Top line	Shock leads to unseeing. In his fright he shuts things out. He should be careful not to panic others. Examining the value of what he has to lose leads to seeing.

Trigrams: Chên, Kên, K'an, Chên.
Thunder (Chên) up the mountain
(Kên) and down the abyss (K'an).
Potential discharge (Chên).

51

Pattern

The world is shaken
to its foundation.
Unparalleled relief
must follow.

Nature

Lightning tears the air
and all beasts cower.
Strikes at the earth
and they tremble.
Its thunder rolls away,
uncovering the sun
and beautiful normality.

Human

Shock follows shock
until his reality
itself is shaken.
Then he will laugh from his belly
at his alarm,
at his escape,
at his relief;
and examine his weaknesses.

Form

Authority stamps,
shaking its power;
and withdraws
creating order.

Moving lines.

A wider view.

Bottom line	He does not prepare more activity, needing quiet to see where he is, what he is.
Second line	Not allowing his feelings to run away with him, he does not let them become fixed. This is an effort, as he would like to follow them but knows they would narrow his view.
Third line	He acts out with his body. Without this his flow would be stifled and his health in danger.
Fourth line	When he seeks a wider view it is not a view of what he does outside. He keeps the outside still to see inside.
Fifth line	He keeps his feelings quietly to himself without difficulty, not identifying his feelings in his situation.
Top line	Accepting inner stillness in the flowing is being in it but not of it. Harmonious in the mature, when identified involvement has been exhausted, for it has a wider reality than that.

Trigrams: Kên, K'an, Chên, Kên.
Inner stillness (Kên) in the
flowing (K'an) discharges its
energy (Chên) by returning to
stillness (Kên).

Pattern

Seeking to return
to a peak once known.
The completion
that contains the beginning.
The start that is the end.

Nature

The low reaches upward.
The confined seeks to spread.
The fruit of the seed
seeks to become seed.

Human

Resisting movement
he avoids beginnings.
Knowing that in the beginning
there was no end
he seeks no end.
Thereby he arrives
at a wider beginning.

Form

Cycles begin and end.
Their beginning and ending
has no ending
and no beginning.
This has the form
of encompassing a wider view.

53 Moving lines.

Persistence.

Bottom line
He does not prepare further persistence, which makes some uncertainty, but he feels an end for the need of endurance, it is not that he fails to persist.

Second line
The end of persistently co-ordinating his feelings. He can at last relax this great effort.

Third line
The ego-self is persistently active, which affects the flow of his relationships. Time to re-examine his own ways.

Fourth line
He seeks to rest between bouts of activity. If there is rest offered this is harmonious, if not he must be prepared to go on.

Fifth line
His emotional acceptance is constant. This gradually makes changes of great benefit in those around him.

Top line
He fulfils himself by persisting in accepting experience as it comes to him.

Trigrams: Kên, K'an, Li, Sun.
Keeping still (Kên) in the flowing
(K'an) means clinging (Li) to the
firm (Sun) amongst opposition
(K'an and Li in the middle
trigrams).

53

Pattern

Clinging to the firm
avoids being swept away.
Allows progress
where there is opposition.

Nature

The tree on the mountain
grows tenaciously,
refusing to be uprooted.

Human

Endurance gives time
for achieving ends.
A presence continued
acquires influence.
Amongst uncertainty
he remains calm and firm.

Form

That which continues,
while changing
to meet circumstances
has the art of endurance.

54 Moving lines.

Held back — breaks forth.

Bottom line
He releases tension through making preparations. This means his release is at some cost, but it is gained.

Second line
Co-ordinating his feelings for a break through, he needs to be single minded to get his feelings expressed. It is important for him to do this.

Third line
When he cannot act out directly, or bring his flow into the necessary outer form, it will flow in some unconventional way — and he need not be downhearted at that.

Fourth line
He accepts that his actions have to be delayed, knowing that they can be accomplished.

Fifth line
Circumstances warrant more trust in the flow than he can feel, his feelings are over-cautious, so he will build up more inner force before trusting that he can move successfully.

Top line
Where are the inner connections by which he knows himself? Disbelieving that he can flow he cannot. Returning to the simple regains the origin of flow.

Trigrams: Tui, Li, K'an, Chên. Emerging joyously (Tui at the bottom), its brightness (Li) is quenched (K'an) by opposition (Li, K'an). Thunder and lightning! (Chên).

54

Pattern

Young and joyful
but shy to venture.
Jumps with both feet.
Becomes an active force.

Nature

The lake flows out,
a young river
reluctant to flow;
coming to an abyss
it turns into a torrent.

Human

His natural flow,
too long held back,
accepts any course
for movement.
Desire long unfulfilled
breaks forth.
How else could it become?

Form

When great force
overcomes unmoving friction
it is suddenly unopposed.

55 Moving lines.

Plentiful relationship.

Bottom line	Preparing action with another that they will complete together in harmony.
Second line	What he needs is there, but he is smothered in distrust. Not co-ordinating his feelings he is confused and acting from this is unharmonious. He will find what he needs when he can trust.
Third line	He needs to act out in his ego-self, but overdoing this damages that relationship on which he relies to act out.
Fourth line	Where the ego path is the basis of relationship the way is difficult; however, equality and respect come from mutually accepting this individual acting out.
Fifth line	His own emotional needs do not govern his relationships. This leaves him free to make numerous fruitful bonds.
Top line	Although he has much to give, it is much to hide. Hiding the wood from the flames creates no warmth.

Trigrams: Li, Sun, Tui, Chên. 55
Emerging fire (Li at the bottom)
meets wood (Sun) so is born
(Tui) into great activity (Chên).

Pattern   The life force finds a form
              which enables it to act plentifully.

Nature   When the fire has fuel
              there is a great blaze.

Human   His energies flow naturally
              into activity.
              What he needs
              comes to hand.
              Acting after maturing
              has abundant success.

Form   The idea
              worked out in privacy
              comes out with an easy force.

Moving lines.

Search for new reality.

Bottom line	He does not prepare fundamental changes so he wanders about in himself and is unsatisfied. Reality is there to choose from, but not to hold.
Second line	His earlier experience serves to make his reality. Holding these feelings close he does not re-combine them in different ways which would give him new realities.
Third line	He is free only so long as he does not fix his state of reality. Continually acting out consumes a range of possibilities which then no longer shelter nor serve him. He needs other modes of being as well as this.
Fourth line	Accepting as his reality the one he is acting out, he possesses it so that it both shelters and encloses him like the shell of an egg.
Fifth line	He takes his own feelings about his reality as only a small part of it. He has hit upon something that will nourish him well, the idea is like a seed that leads him on to many things.
Top line	He tries believing his reality is limited to what it seems. This makes it static and it is soon consumed, so his relief at solving this problem is short-lived. He has lost the flow of his nourishment, which is the dynamic flow of changing reality.

Trigrams: Kên, Sun, Tui, Li.
When the mountain (Kên) is
wooded (Sun) it gives birth (Tui)
to fire (Li).

 56

Pattern   Stillness and maturity
                searching for the new
                leads to continual change.

Nature   When it is very dry
                fire ranges across the forest
                looking always for new fuel.

Human   He goes from place to place
                making changes in each:
                searching his death
                that will enable him to live,
                searching a change in himself.

Form   The state
                engulfs other states
                when its own opposition is dead.

Moving lines.

Where is identity?

Bottom line	It is difficult to grasp firmly that his wholeness includes his separateness. He needs to go into separateness and return to wholeness many times before he can have his identity in both together.
Second line	Having his identity in feeling and layers of symbolic meaning widens his awareness.
Third line	He narrows when he feels his identity in separateness. When this narrow reality is cut off from the whole it repeats itself to exhaustion.
Fourth line	Not accepting his identity in separateness he seeks other realities and is rewarded and nourished by a living, dynamic reality.
Fifth line	He makes his identity in many variable ways of feeling (at the mid-point between inner and outer) and moves freely amongst continual change.
Top line	Making his identity in his inner reality he loses his ability to act outside, and his sense of belonging there. It does not expand his reality to exchange it for another.

The firm (Sun) gives birth (Tui)
to transient brightness (Li) which
clings to the firm (Sun).

Pattern   The mature,
            the more knit together,
            starts to fragment,
            but returns to wholeness.

Nature   Creation has separateness.
            It hungers for wholeness.
            Taking part is this food.

Human   He sees his flame.
            His independence kindles him.
            Separation knows a lesser reality
            and clings
            to its part in the whole.

            His outer ego
            is the size of his separateness.

Form   The part serves the whole
            when it knows it is itself
            yet inseparable.

Moving lines.

It comes!

Bottom line — Forming a way of expression. He has the power and so expresses harmoniously.

Second line — He co-ordinates his feelings towards what comes and is in tune with it.

Third line — Although it comes he does not act it out. He holds it for a future time and has not the joy of flowing.

Fourth line — Seeking joy he cannot find it. Taking his individual flow of expression as his prime reality he loses the necessary spontaneity.

Fifth line — What comes is change and cannot be held. He focuses his feelings about what comes: these, like falling leaves of a tree are a passing effect, he cannot hold them.

Top line — When he does not experience his life flow as his reality, he needs stimulation from the world to feel joy: he constantly seeks stimulation.

Trigrams: Tui, Li, Sun, Tui.
Intuitions (Tui) of brightness (Li)
become firm, confirmed (Sun)
returning brightness and joy (Tui).

Pattern   The pre-form of activity
has joy.
The formed activity also
has joy.

Nature   A sunrise that excites the soul.
A day that satisfies it.

Human   He knows in his fibre
the power to create.
He knows in his body
the motions of creation.
How could he not
enjoy his creation?

Form   The prototype is ready.
The plan is made.
Harmonious with its outcome.

59 Moving lines.

Dissipation of energy.

Bottom line   He does not prepare new activities for
              his energy; he harnesses it to whatever
              is going forward, which is harmonious.

Second line   Providing for himself a necessary security
              by following his feelings gives relief from
              frustration.

Third line   He restrains his individual acting out.
              By making less of himself he is less subject
              to being drained.

Fourth line   By not accepting his part in a dissipating
              situation he divides himself from it, which
              brings him strength.

Fifth line   He accepts the ways of others by allowing
              the dissipation of his own feelings about
              his way. This does not lessen him.

Top line   He accepts dissipation of the situation
              he is in. His flow of life force is no
              longer in it so it is harmonious to leave it.

Emerging from the depth (K'an)
potential discharge (Chên) up the
slope (Kên) becomes gentle (Sun).

Pattern   Energy
               working against a resistance
               is dissipated.

Nature   Thunder roars
               in the low land,
               but is hardly heard
               up the mountain.

Human   The task
               is beyond his powers.
               If he is wise
               he seeks help
               or goes other ways.

Form   When resistance
               overcomes activity
               systems lose their cohesion.

Moving lines.

Scarcity.

Bottom line	Like a plant in drought he grows more roots and needs less leaves. Having but little life flow, he prepares how he will use it.
Second line	Using his feelings in a time of scarcity he needs to co-operate in relationships or his feelings will become sour.
Third line	If he acted out the path would soon peter out, so he holds back.
Fourth line	It is harmonious that he accepts not acting out in a time of scarcity.
Fifth line	Co-ordinating in harmonious relationships gives a time of scarcity also a fullness.
Top line	He does not see the scarcity and his resources run out. He learns from this.

Trigrams: Tui, Chên, Kên, K'an.
Emerging like a bud (Tui), active
as thunder and lightning (Chên),
made as still as a mountain peak
(Kên), falling to the abyss (K'an).

Pattern
When there is little
at the beginning
its activity rises to a peak,
its limit,
and falls to a dangerous low.

Nature
In poor soil
the seed germinates,
rises up,
but does not mature.

Human
He limits flow.
Seeing scarcity,
spreads resources
to avoid famine.

Form
When the little
is gathered up by the few,
the rest are empty.
This is dangerous.

61 Moving lines.

Awareness of wider reality.

Bottom line
When inner and outer are in harmony the inner preparations for activity are felt literally throughout. If his outer awareness is too involved there, however, it mistakes the need and possesses it.

Second line
His deep inner world flows outward through his feelings and quenches his thirst.

Third line
He does not now act out on an individual path, being aware of the one-sided nature of this. He sees polarities as equally valid and uses first one side of the coin then the other. He no longer hides half, or fears the other.

Fourth line
When he ceases to recognize his outer image as himself he loses the driving power that this identification creates. Also he no longer needs it.

Fifth line
When he finds his symbol-forming feelings to be his reality he stands at a doorway looking both in and out. It is the heart of his life.

Top line
Awareness of his inner self does not reach waking consciousness directly, but through the medium of symbolic feeling. Knowing it is there is the meaning of faith; turning that knowing into some perception of it he fools himself with his own images.

Trigrams: Tui, Chên, Kên, Sun.
The bud emerges (Tui), breaks
forth (Chên) up a slope to a peak
(Kên) of firm maturity (Sun).

Pattern

Flowing in and out
of activity
is harmonious.
Contact and awareness
between inner and outer
has strength.

Nature

The bud unfolds,
opens to opposites,
enclosing both in seed.

Human

He finds it easy
to know his inner truths,
to flow between his
inner-outer life
and feel more whole.

Form

A new dimension becomes real
when inner and outer connect
to become one feeling.

Moving lines.

After reaching a level.

Bottom line | If he acts he will be unprepared. He needs
care if taking off in new directions.

Second line | He is guided by his feelings more as though by
another person because he is not identified in
them. To know where he is he needs to co-ordinate
his feeling into that knowledge.

Third line | He acts out as though his level were a personal
attribute. Not facing his inner awareness he
risks losing it.

Fourth line | He accepts a new personal awareness. How will
he use it? Any advantage he may now see risks
externalizing his awareness; he would then lose
sight of its source. If he appears to gain he
will lose.

Fifth line | He holds back his flow by not accepting his
subjective feelings about his position.
Identifying his level with rank impairs his
inner awareness.

Top line | He is not recognizing a wider awareness that
is latent in him. He misses a chance of taking
off in a new direction.

Emerging without activity (Kên),
already firm and formed (Sun).
Buds (Tui) into new activity
(Chên).

Pattern

Action has given birth
to stillness, consolidation.
From this
small new movement can arise.

Nature

The wood of the tree
is solid and firm.
New growth from this
is a small part
of the whole.

Human

His ideas are formed.
Through these
changes push their way,
so he changes
but a little.

Form

The establishment
is not the origin
of social change.

63 Moving lines.

Completion.

Bottom line | By preparing for a new cycle of experience
he removes the driving force from the old,
so the end of this becomes disorganized.

Second line | When he does not gather his feelings around
a new situation he is open to influence from
outside. This is only a hangover from
completing something, when this is gone he will
have his usual control.

Third line | Starting the day vigorously cleaning out his
room, he is not satisfied until he has rearranged
the furniture. If he has joy in his mind,
not resentment, it will go well.

Fourth line | Not accepting that completion means a change
of experience, he clothes his new actions as
he did the old and is confused.

Fifth line | Accepting changing feelings. If he does this
too soon and too fulsomely it is less harmonious
than if he allows events to appear to change
his feelings.

Top line | If he does not accept that one cycle is ended
and another beginning events will overtake him,
and may submerge him if he continues like this.

Trigrams: Li, K'an, Li, K'an. 63
Fire emerges (Li). Water acts
(K'an). Fire acts (Li). Water
returns (K'an).

Pattern   Fire enters water.
Water enters fire.
Mutually they change
each other's reality,
forming what is different
after they have changed.

Nature   Under the sun.
Through the sea.
The reality of rock
is sand.

Human   He may be surprised
to find himself
without the thing he has made
with such care.
He can rejoice the passing
from one reality to another.

Form   Complete change is an end
and a beginning.

Moving lines.

Incomplete change.

Bottom line   He does not prepare (choose) a dynamic,
              changing reality for himself, taking the
              lead of others.

Second line   Co-ordinating his feelings towards change.
              When he closely co-ordinates one end with
              another beginning, there is difficulty in
              ending and beginning afresh, but this can
              be worked through.

Third line   He cannot complete his acting out in the
              old way. He needs a basic change in order
              to act harmoniously.

Fourth line   By making a jump he would change suddenly
              into rewarding harmony. He may do this
              because he recognizes incomplete change.

Fifth line   By not being concerned with his feelings
              about his situation he works his way out of it.

Top line   By accepting incomplete change as the reality
              of his situation he relaxes his tensions, but
              if he accepts it totally as his reality he
              cannot lead himself out of it.

Trigrams: K'an, Li, K'an, Li.
Water emerges (K'an). Fire acts
(Li). Water acts (K'an). Fire
returns (Li).

64

Pattern — Change is not complete.
Only part is changed.

Nature — Water enters fire,
evaporates,
leaving fire.

Human — He starts out into opposition.
He is so changed
he opposes no more.

Form — When the existing order
can change its challengers
partial changes occur.

LOWER TRIGRAMS	UPPER TRIGRAMS							
	Ch'ien ☰	Chên ☳	K'an ☵	Kên ☶	K'un ☷	Sun ☴	Li ☲	Tui ☱
Ch'ien ☰	1	34	5	26	11	9	14	43
Chên ☳	25	51	3	27	24	42	21	17
K'an ☵	6	40	29	4	7	59	64	47
Kên ☶	33	62	39	52	15	53	56	31
K'un ☷	12	16	8	23	2	20	35	45
Sun ☴	44	32	48	18	46	57	50	28
Li ☲	13	55	63	22	36	37	30	49
Tui ☱	10	54	60	41	19	61	38	58

KEY TO THE HEXAGRAM NUMBERS